PLAY IT
FULL

7 STEPS TO UNLOCK YOUR EXTRAORDINARY CAREER

May this book be your best partner
in your journey to joy & fulfillment.

Shilpa Kulshrestha

Kapil Kulshrestha

PLAY IT FULL

7 STEPS TO UNLOCK YOUR EXTRAORDINARY CAREER

written by

SHILPA KULSHRESTHA

&

KAPIL KULSHRESHTHA

ADHYYAN / BOOKS

© Shilpa Kulshrestha & Kapil Kulshreshtha

Play It Full

1st Edition
All rights reserved
Publication Date: October 2019
Price: ₹999 | USD $19.95 | AUD $24.95
ISBN: 978-93-88644-38-9

Published by:
Adhyyan Books
Office No. 637,
Opposite Vivanta by Taj,
DDA SFS. Pocket-1, Dwarka,
Sec-22, New Delhi-110077, India
Website: http://adhyyanbooks.com
E-mail: contact@adhyyanbooks.com

Dedication

Dear Sanya and Elina,

The biggest outcome for us during the writing this book has been you two stepping up your own game in such a short time.

The incredible partnership and thinking that this book has created between the four of us is beyond words.

Play It Full,

Mum & Dad

Thank you Grant Cardone for your guidance during the 10X bootcamp in Sydney 2019. This book would not have been possible but for you.

The Guiding Philosophy in this Book

"Each human being is born to stand TALL, be healthy and wealthy in mind, body & spirit."

This Book is our promise to make you 2mm TALLER!

– Shilpa and Kapil

What Others Are Saying

"This book deals with the most important issue of our time... knowing thyself. If you are looking to achieve more personal success and happiness, this book is for you."

– Benjamin J Harvey
Co-founder of Authentic Education, Australia

"Even if you have read other career growth books earlier, you will find the insights in this book as intuitive, practical, and authentic - as these are from the authors' own first hand experiences. The insightful pages here will engage you, force you to reflect, provide you with tools, and energise you to take actions to change the gears of your career."

– Jagdish Belwal
CIO of an MNC, and ex CIO Tata Motors

"Achieving outstanding results in your career is possible only if there is a structured and focused path you can follow. By empowering you to identify and eliminate your challenges, this book sets up such a system, and will be with you forever."

– Reyna Matthes
Women in Leadership Expert, Sydney

"Very different from the tactics often promoted through popular self-improvement literature, this book concentrates on a strategic thought-through framework to accelerate your personal development and your career."

– Dr John Burgin
C-level Tech Executive, Sydney

"Finally, a book that covers A to Z on career transformation in a simple way that can be implemented by anyone wanting to get out of an average career!"

- Ramendra Verma
Business Head of a global Big Four Consulting Company, India

"The beauty of this book lies in the simplicity of the message it sends. How often do we fall foul of things that are obvious and in plain sight? If only we could open our minds to think with a new mindset. Kapil and Shilpa have a powerful message in these words."

– Roger La Salle
CEO Rudders RLS - Matrix Thinking", Melbourne

"I love this book so much and it's got me thinking on a deeper level about winning more. It will help you create powerhouse measurable results for your life and career. Great read."

– Edward Zia
Marketing Mentor CPM & Master Coach, Sydney

"If you want to discover how you can break out of the current mould in your career, this book is for you. It will change the trajectory of your career and your life forever."

– Rajeev John
Business Head, India based FMCG MNC, India

"If you ever wanted to get out of the average game in your career and achieve extraordinary results, this is the book for you. This is a must read for anyone who is serious about making it big in their corporate life."

– Sanjeev Honakhande
Client Partner, A fortune 200 company, London

"86% people are not engaged with their work. This book will easily cut it to half. Every organisation should keep this in their shelf for employees to start finding their personal best."

– Ashok Kumar Thambi
Senior Leader, Large IT Services MNC, New York

"Play It Full Out/ Play It Full is a great read for creating maximum impact across all professions and speaks to the global audience of today. It will snap you out of the monotonous pattern of your daily life and dissolve the barriers that are limiting your growth."

– Sajeev Menon
Cyber Security Risk Consultant and Centium Group, Sydney

Warnings of losses you will sustain after finishing this book

This book will make you lose a lot of stuff. You are likely to lose some friends, but do not worry, only those who were never committed to your growth in the first place.

You will lose the boredom you have felt in your job.

Many of you will lose your willingness to wear a t-shirt with someone else's name. Your focus will shift to creating your greatness so that you can wear your own name on that t-shirt.

You will also lose a lot of damaging beliefs you have held in the past as you work through this book. Another loss will be those behaviours that were creating massive pain and self-sabotage for you.

And we assure you, if you implement the strategies laid out in this book, you will certainly lose some of the weight you have been carrying on your shoulders for years.

We can promise you; things will not be the same once you start to forget the days when you weren't clear about the direction in your life.

Some of you will lose some of the money lying dormant in your bank as you start investing in your personal growth at a pace you have never felt before and make unimaginable amount of wealth.

Most importantly, you will lose your mediocre mindset, which will pave the way for creating outstanding wins in life and **you will stand TALL like never before!**

Contents

What does this book contain?

"We can't solve problems by using the same kind of thinking we used when we created them."

—Albert Einstein

In June 2018, Mexicans jumping in jubilation shook the ground hard enough to set off earthquake detectors. People danced in the streets after their team scored a surprise victory over the World Cup defending champion Germany. The Institute of Geological and Atmospheric Investigations even said that some highly sensitive earthquake sensors registered tremors at two sites in the capital of Mexico seven seconds after the game's 35th minute!

On 23rd Jan 2016, we were present at the Sydney Cricket Grounds, when the Indian cricket team won the T20 against Australia. As we saw the stadium erupt in chaos as the nail-biting match reached it's last over, we found our own energy reaching new heights. The jubilance and celebration around were deafening!

We are sure that you feel a surge of energy just reading this! However, the passion you have around your favourite team winning is hardly carried through in your own life. Your life has probably been lived in a series of peaks, but with majority of your time spent reacting to the circumstances around you and making sense of this mad, mad, mad world as you chase success.

This book is all about how you can play it full in your life to achieve the wildest of your career dreams. It is about giving you an unbeatable mindset about your own capabilities. This book is also about how you can have your cake and eat it too.

There is a reason we love books.

The richness of books comes from being able to tap into the vast experiences of someone else, their wisdom in a specific area of interest, their in-depth research and the life of the people they know. It is quite intriguing how everything is made available to the reader in a few hours of a focused read.

This is one such book!

Our entire focus is on sharing our combined experience of 4 decades, our wisdom from thousands of hours of trainings that we have done in a highly immersive environment with the likes of Tony Robbins, Grant Cardone, Dan Lok, Gary Vaynerchuk, Brandon Burchard, Robin Sharma, Vishen Lakhani, Ben Harvey and Cham Tang- to name a few.

Our strategy in this book is based on our learnings from these strategists, coaches and mentors, which we have further fine-tuned based on our experiences in real life, which come from enabling our mentees to produce extraordinary results in their life and career.

And we have brought all of this out in the most authentic form possible, and in easy, bite-sized pieces for you to consume.

This book is focused on YOU.

It is focused on giving you the tips, learnings, and mindset changes needed not only to get to that next promotion or career change- but also to reach a path that you can follow on your own, as you go forward in life.

What makes it even more amazing is that as life partners, as business partners and co-authors, we have challenged each other to put only high impact items into this book.

It is a tall claim to make. Yes, we know.

But this is exactly what we are offering you, as our beloved reader, who is trusting us to make an impact in his/her life.

We promise we will hold your trust and bring YOU results, provided you do all exercises as you read through this book, with a focus, drive and hunger to transform your life.

This book will change your perspective on how you approach your career by helping you get an insight into what it takes to beat the average mindset and become outstanding in your career.

This book answers questions related to:

Career Growth

- How do I get promoted faster?

- What if I need to make a career change?

- How do I earn more money doing what I do or by changing my career?

- How do I get to a more senior role?

- How do I make myself wanted so that I can get more money, status and fulfilment?

- How do I handle my non-cooperative manager?

Career Direction

- How do I find a direction in my career?

- How do I get clarity around what I want to do?

- What do I need to do so that I can move forward with great speed?

Handling Obstacles in Life:

- How do I answer difficult questions such as:

  o Are my skills in demand or am I getting rusty?

  o What are the knowledge gaps and how do I fill them up fast?

  o Am I too old?

  o Am I too young?

- How do I handle office politics and negative environments?

- How do I handle extreme and ongoing work pressures?

- How do I handle my personal constraints such as:

  o Confidence

  o Communication abilities

  o Low self-esteem

  o Financial pressure

  o Getting more discipline around my life

  o Stopping self-sabotaging behaviour

  o Become consistent in life

- o Make right decisions in my career

- o Get more focus

- o Overthinking

- o Conviction

- How do I sell myself better within the organisation?

- How do I portray myself outside the organisation I work for?

- How can I multitask and take care of all the priorities I have?

- How do I get the flexibility I want and still be a star?

The book is divided into 3 key parts.

Part 1: Awareness – understanding the current

Part 2: Solution Components – Career Architecture

Part 3: Detailed Solution

Part 1 contains 2 chapters

Chapter 1 talks about HOW DO WE DO THINGS CURRENTLY and the issues with that. This chapter is geared towards developing an understanding of our motivation in life and how do we operate generally.

A deep understanding of this is really critical since any solution otherwise will be tactical and doomed to fail. We will talk about the issues with a distorted understanding of what it takes to be successful in the corporate environment.

Chapter 2 talks about WHY WE DO WHAT WE DO. It is important to understand our deep-rooted beliefs and reasons as to how we operate currently. Here we also look into self-imposed obstacles and how do they impact our decisions in life.

Part 2 contains 1 chapter

Chapter 3 contains the KEY SOLUTION COMPONENTS that create building blocks for a powerful career. An understanding of them is intellectually possible should the reader choose to ignore Chapter 1 and 2 but implementation of these will not lead to expected results unless issues identified in 1 and 2 are removed.

Part 3 contains 1 chapter

Chapter 4 contains the solution based on OUR 7-STEP PROCESS and how it needs to be executed in your life. A reader may be tempted to jump on it and read it right away but the benefit of this will not be much, as this will just turn out to be plain intellectual knowledge and not easy to do unless you go through the prior chapters and do the exercises mentioned in a systematic way.

The remaining 2 chapters provide closure and the next steps, you must take to start living powerfully.

As avid readers ourselves, we are keen to provide you workable strategies and not just another idea generating book.

Here is our big promise to you. Reading these chapters in the order they are written will take you through a structured, thought provoking process, which will produce extraordinary results in your career and help you play it full.

However, there is always something amazing.

There is a hidden gem in this book. If you read it the way it is meant to be read, you will find it and it will leave you in awe of your own capacity and clarity around what you can accomplish. It is possible that you will have to read it twice or even, thrice to find it, but when you do — you will definitely see everything in your career change wonderfully and irrevocably.

Authors' Note

The last couple of years have been a bit of a roller coaster ride for our family as we took a 180-degree pivot in our life. We left our successful corporate career of 4 decades and started a new journey.

2017 marked the start of our journey as mindset coaches, enabling people to make conscious choices in their life and career. Over these years, we have jointly read over 500 books, attended over 20 highly immersive and highly ticketed programs, attended 60+ online programs and been coached every week by people who started their own journey before we did and are making an outstanding life for themselves.

Some of these days were spent experiencing a lot of adrenaline rush, pacing in the backyard, planning for hours until midnight, with the moon by our side, vetting our intentions. Then there were those low moments, when we reminded each other of the support we had and with every hurdle we crossed, we truly felt like a power couple.

It was somewhere during this journey that we decided to eliminate the word "problem" from our vocabulary and replace it with the word "hurdle"- as hurdles are meant to be crossed. With each hurdle, we slowed down, gathered ourselves and went across with all our might. Our life went through a series of massive changes.

This journey has been truly transformational for us and our daughters as they witnessed our struggles, the fight for our conviction, our value system, setting up a vision and achieving our goals one by one. Their support and contribution to our dream can never be underestimated and we will never be able to thank them enough for their understanding and unconditional love.

As Elena Cardone says "It is not WHAT milestone you meet, but WHO you become in the journey that matters the most."

As we got stronger with each win, the creative juices started to flow and we decided to pen down all our learnings, which we believe will add value to anyone looking at not just fast-tracking their career- but doing it in a way that is sustainable and with clarity.

We have had our share of an average life - and becoming mediocre is the worst thing we have ever experienced.

This started our war with mediocrity, because most people stuck in that state do not even know that they are playing an average game. But we learnt that it is not hard to get out of it!

We believe that being able to choose is the greatest gift we have as humans. The power of making conscious choices in life is at the fundamental core of this book. At the end of it, you will know, feel and act in ways you have never done before and the conscious choices you make in your life will create a career which is built on top of your personal power.

This book is our effort to push you to think differently, check where you stand today, break your limiting beliefs and unchain yourselves to claim your spot to fly high in the open sky.

-   Shilpa Kulshrestha and Kapil Kulshreshtha: co-authors, partners and conscious choice coaches.

Introduction

Kapil: It was a cold August morning in Sydney and it was about to be one of my best days. I was about to do the part of my job I loved the most. I was going to inform one of my colleagues that he had been promoted to a Senior Manager.

He had done an outstanding job with a client and had really made a big difference to their major initiative of a rewrite of their core applications. The revenue growth in the account wouldn't have been possible without him.

As I reached the office for the 9:00 am meeting, I saw a text that he will be 10 min late due to his daily stand-up meeting going overtime.

I went to the cafeteria downstairs, ordered my favourite cappuccino and started to wait.

Tod (name changed) soon arrived with his usual smile and found me sipping my coffee. He declined my invitation for coffee and sat down in front of me. We got down to the usual chit chat and I got all the information about how things were moving and how he was confident about continuing growth at the client's end.

While I was hooked on to his every word, especially as he laid out the plans for making the most impact in a new area, I found it difficult to hold my own enthusiasm and soon told him that he had been promoted to the Senior Manager position.

What happened next was completely unexpected. I never saw it coming.

Tears started rolling down his cheeks!

I sat there, dumbfounded, trying to make sense of what was happening. Seeing him crying with his head between his hands, the odd looks from people around me was adding to my surprise on why this news would make someone act in that way!

After a few minutes, which seemed like eternity to me, Tod finally recovered.

Without waiting for me to ask, something I was really thankful I didn't have to, Tod started sharing how he had waited for this for years.

Within 2 months of joining this large company 7 years ago, he was quickly labelled as a star performer by his managers, peers and onsite leads.

During appraisal time however, he was not given the highest rating band. His manager confided in him that due to a limited number of "top bucket" level ratings, someone else had to be promoted that year – and even when she didn't believe that the other person deserved that higher rating.

While it did not make any sense to Tod, he accepted it as a piece of corporate wisdom.

The second year, he got the top bucket rating and his manager told him, "you are on your way up".

A few months later, when promotions were announced in the conference room, Tod had to hold back his tears again. This manager told him that since he was not given two continuous highest band ratings in the last 2 years, there was no way he could be promoted.

When he spoke about missing the top band the year before as someone else was to be promoted, the manager simply feigned ignorance of having said that!

Tod was a fighter, a star performer and a very committed guy, so he accepted it as his fate.

"Looking back, I should have left then", he shared his regret with me.

Continuing his story, he laid out how in the third year, the same manager regrettably informed him that while he had continuous high bucket rating for last 2 years, the quota for promotion was very low and many people had spent a longer time than him or were onsite or some other inexplicable reason as to why he had to miss out.

The manager told him that when the salary increase happens, he will definitely take care of Tod- and he did give Tod an extra 3% increase. Others got 7%, but Tod got 10%.

"This seemed like a good deal at the time, as I felt that my work was noticed and I was given a privileged treatment- but I didn't realise that the noose would continue to tighten", he retorted, "I definitely should have left".

Another 3-4 months later, his manager quit and a new person became his manager from another business unit.

He was very apprehensive as he got his yearly performance rating, that this manager decided based on working with him for barely 4 months. He was not in the top band that he consistently was at for the last 2 years.

Angrily, he confronted his manager but was put back in his place as a list of his behavioural challenges was thrown at him.

"You don't really speak in meetings"

"You don't mix with people much"

"You really have to be able to sell yourself. Look at XYZ, on how well he does it"

This person had ignored the point that he consistently got the highest band in the previous 2 years.

The manager also didn't consider that Todd was an introvert by nature. This manager was judging him based on his own personal standards of how an excellent performer should be.

Sensing that things could only get worse, Tod sought out another role under a good manager and moved to a different business unit.

This made the year 4 promotion opportunity pass by.

By this time, things had gone bad at home as well – as his father constantly reminded him how others were doing better than him. He even felt at times that his wife was prodding him to spend more time at office so that he can become better at his work.

Losing respect from his own family really hit him hard.

The 5th year, he didn't even bother asking for a promotion as his performance had gone down and he barely managed to hold on to the second level of rating.

Tod knew there was no hope and started looking out for an onsite assignment to help pay the house loan he had taken in anticipation of an increased salary. He soon moved onsite and, it felt great that he was making good money.

The promotion stopped being a priority and he only concerned himself in ensuring he saved as much as he could and sent the money home.

Tod definitely made a great use of that time, as he loved the change and client office environment, which became his only focus.

As Tod finished his story, I was stuck by a dreadful feeling that he actually considered his promotion as a **favour!**

How strange that a perfectly capable and great performer had been turned into a cynical, resigned and average performer within a few years!

This is a true story that happened in 2015. It was a very painful moment for me, as I questioned my own allegiance to that company and the culture this comparative performance appraisal system represented. The hopes and dreams Tod had and how year after year, they were shattered. What I dislike most about this is the fact that **he allowed his life to be controlled by other people.**

====

While every single element of Tod's story is not going to be applicable to you, there are elements we know that you can relate to.

Think about it, when was the last time you had to go through something that clearly was unfair?

It is likely that you feel deeply in control of your decisions.

However, let us do this small exercise.

Ask these questions to yourself:

A. What are your 3 top-most accomplishments in life?

B. What resulted in those accomplishments?

C. Who did you most depend on in those situations?

The vast majority of people respond to these questions with a clarity that it was their own actions coupled with their own conviction, that led to those accomplishments.

Let us consider a different angle.

Write down the list of 10 life changing decisions **you have taken** in your life, where you were truly in control and you made a conscious choice to do it differently.

Most people will find it very hard to write more than 5.

This is because we often have a mindset of **"let me flow freely in this river of life"**.

It is like having fifty cans of soda every day and allowing the "free flow" argument to rationalise it - and eventually letting it impact your life in irreversible ways.

The problem with this "free flow" idea is that it is reactive in nature. It is based on what is in front of you at this very moment. It lacks direction.

Life is like a river continuously flowing downstream.

The free flow folks, just want that easy going life, where they move with the current, bending in this direction, going in that direction, giving in to whatever path it takes, occasionally making those decisions that takes them to a different route, till one steep flow makes them pick up speed and ultimately crash on a rock.

A basic human survival instinct then makes them fight hard to get back in the flow, till there is a next time when a series of incidences find them crashing on different rocks time and time again.

Being able to choose is about constantly anticipating the bend, adjusting the speed, flowing with the current for a little while, enjoying the view but keeping an eye on the direction and speed.

That is when the journey becomes fun. That is when the journey becomes invigorating. That is when the journey becomes an opportunity to play it full every day, when you have control on how to respond to whatever comes in the way- being proactive rather than reactive.

That is true mindfulness.

Ask yourself, is life for you more of just survival? Or are you actually playing it full?

While you have had peaks in your career, those peaks were probably more a result of saving yourselves from the disaster at the next wave or bend and not from having instincts that you develop when you make conscious choices in life.

There are other reasons why you need to get started on playing it full.

A giant wave of technology advancement is coming our way. A study by McKinsey Global Institute estimates that 400 to 800 million jobs will be automated by 2030.

What are you doing to get future ready? Are you busy evaluating if your job will be affected or are you on your front foot creating alternatives for yourselves? Or, are you thinking that you will be too old by then?

As per a paper from Singularity University, for every year you live between now and 2036, your average age will increase by 3 months each year. This means by 2036, the average age will be 92 years.

Post that, for every year you live, the average age will increase by 1 more year. Therefore, if you are 40-years-old, by the time you die, the average age is likely to be 127 years. And you may just overshoot it by 15 years! 142 years of age!

The number looks crazy and too old to be true. However, consider that if someone was told 100 years back that the average age will almost double, they would have had same scepticism as you currently have.

As a matter of fact, there is no comparison. There was a great book, "The Red Queen" by Matt Ridley, where the author pointed out that no matter how fast medical technology grows, the diseases catch up fast. We are not outside that race. The combined impact of Nano-technology, medical technology, connectivity, artificial intelligence means that within the next 5 years, a lot of current human killer diseases will be thing of the past. The top 5 of these include heart diseases, cancer and strokes. These will become things of the past! Of the 53 million people that die each year, a whopping 23 million are killed due to these diseases: so imagine these getting wiped off from the list of diseases!

Some may say that some other creature may take over – but if so, those creatures will definitely not have this high of a fatality rate.

Like it or not, YOU are going to live a long and strong life.

You may as well start planning to.

This book is about developing those muscles in your head, so that you can start living an awesome life.

The way to develop those instincts is by making deliberate efforts to become a person who can anticipate the bends. A person who can get out of the water at will and stand on the rocks to survey the scene in front and then plunge into the icy cold water, knowing fully well what is to be done before the next bend comes.

Is that the kind of person you want to be? Someone who is in control of his career? Someone who is highly sought after for what they have to offer?

But more importantly,

Someone whose strengths are in sync with how the world sees them, and who is constantly able to progress forward by adding value and allowing others to leverage them?

PART 1

Chapter 1
Our Current Mindset

"A problem appropriately identified is a problem 50% solved"

There is one thing which everyone, no matter what profession they are in, has in common - We ALL want to make significant strides in life!

However, a painfully large majority of us are not engaged in fulfilling jobs, work or anywhere close to living our potential.

Why is it so difficult feel to energised to jump out of bed every single day? What stops people from doing that?

While each of us have those moments, most of us find it painfully impossible to love what we do every single moment. A lot of us know people, public figures such as Richard Branson, who live a full life at every moment – but choose to consider them as "exceptional" and therefore give ourselves reasons to not duplicate it in our own lives.

Before we start looking at the solution, let us focus on identifying the real problem, as to what it is that is holding us back.

THE CORPORATE BEAST

Majority of us spend more than a third of our day and more than half of our waking hours at our workplace. We not only have to deal with all the challenges of the corporate environment, but also deal with having to live without the best outcome that we truly deserve.

It will take an entire book to cover every single corporate behaviour. Therefore, we want to cover the core ones that end up defining the problem space, which we can then attack and solve.

Let us jump right into how we operate in a corporate environment.

Workplace Behaviour- Masks We Wear- Where do we hide us?

> *"Are you ok?": always the same question*
> *"I'm fine.": always the same lie*

"I can't believe my boss said this to me!"

"I have done so much for this company and this is how they repay me?"

"My manager is a dumbass, a highly biased, discriminatory person!"

"I can easily replace my manager; she doesn't do anything"

There is a great chance that you are guilty of saying one or more of the above, or similar, at some point in your career.

There are MANY other forms of these victim type statements that we repeat over and over again, when we face serious issues at work or in life. While we talk about others and make them apparently wrong, we are actually harming ourselves quite irreversibly, as instead of looking inward for the cause of our pain, we are looking outward.

Why do we engage in this kind of self-sabotaging behaviour?

Why does our carefully constructed idea of self-worth, values and control on our lives fall apart at the slightest provocation?

Is it because we set fairly high standards for other's behaviours at the workplace and low for ourselves? Or is it because we are surrounded by managers who take some kind of sadistic pleasure in torturing us? Or is it because we absolutely cannot understand our peers and managers – despite sometimes, spending YEARS with them?

Or because we just... suck at handling failures and setbacks at our work place?

The crux of this is that the typical organisational set up most of us work in has a "fit-in" culture rather than a "be-yourself" ideology.

There is an expectation as to how an organisation culture and environment has to be. While HR Leaders and other executives in the companies make their best effort to interpret it for people, the very idea that there is a need to *interpret* it, creates a problem.

When we start working at a young age, we are filled with the promises and are really passionate about the opportunities we have.

Joining 'that one company' and working there becomes a dream come true. We want to really shine and the measurable outcomes are usually in the form of recognition, great appraisal ratings and the monetary benefits.

This continues till there is that one inevitable screwup, we all have gone through it. And the reaction of peers and managers may not come out to be as demeaning as we assume it to be. However, the high standards we hold ourselves to, often make the screwup look like a lightning strike.

And then comes the dreaded time for the appraisal. The infamous bell curve is still very real in some large organisations. People are pitted against each other – their entire work is brought down to a single number and it impacts almost everything – promotion, type of projects, visibility, recognition and even relationships!

We have heard it repeated throughout our careers by literally everyone who is unhappy with the rating, salary increase or for not being recognised adequately.

The stakes are so high!! No wonder majority of people going through that just build up "good" reasons for why they didn't get what they deserved.

They look for clues in their conversation with their managers to validate their feeling "that this was not because of ME"– and then latch on to the one word or one phrase that makes them feel better – even if this usually is a ruse by the manager to just get out of the situation.

Most managers suck at appraisals and would say anything to get out of an uncomfortable situation!

What happens after that to most people, is the dampening of that enthusiasm, the feeling of betrayal and in desperation of being successful, they get lost by looking at the "successful" people, trying to emulate their **behaviours** rather than being who they actually ARE.

This "what it takes to be successful in an organization" is a beast with a billion looks and carries a different interpretation for each one of us. This becomes a very damaging cultural element in large organisations with out-of-date policies, where culture is not owned up by every single person – but is considered to be something driven by HR or senior leadership.

For an individual – with a relatively simple life – this beast shows up as **one-and-the-only-way to be successful.**

The moment that realization sets in, we start to wear a mask to fit in. Through the years, new masks keep stacking up on our face one by one and the vision keeps getting clouded.

We then see our corporate world and our role there through these masks. No wonder the view becomes so distorted and frustrating. Wearing these masks makes it impossible to carry our true self to the work place.

Consider this, you are in a meeting and a super-performer that everyone looks up to walks in. There is a sudden urge in your mind to see how this person is operating. You start thinking about how they walk, how they speak, where they intervene and how they take charge very naturally.

Like it or not, there is a great chance that you will subconsciously start copying that style. In the short term, it works to your advantage as you may find that it helps you connect with people better. However, in the long term, it is massively damaging – if this becomes your dominant style to connect, without any context and content backing it up.

What it means is, once you have connected, what next? How are you going to continue the conversation and connection?

You need content for it and that cannot be copied unfortunately.

It is ironic that the successful people we tend to emulate subconsciously, actually act in accordance with who they truly are.

These amazingly driven individuals, who achieve great things, are just being themselves. And many of us, who want to be that successful end up copying their style and don't get anywhere!

It is a hard truth to digest but unfortunately is a highly repeated pattern in corporate behaviours.

Let us look at it from another angle. Consider your best work so far. Looking back, you know that at the time, the praise and recognition didn't act as a major incentive to that excellence but was a very well-deserved **output**.

Being promoted was not what you were driven by. That is not why you worked hard. You put in your best at the time, because you loved the work or the environment or something that connected you to the cause.

Shilpa: During the exit interview for one of the jobs I quit, my reason for quitting was that, "I cannot feel aligned with the cause any longer" – as I saw my work as something that didn't appeal to my value system.

And yet, isn't that opposite of how you mostly want from work– Promotion, Recognition, Money!

There are clear options here –

A. **Continue to wear that mask –**

This approach creates short-term monetary success, good position/designation but creates a massive conflict within yourself. Yet, you may find hardly any pleasure as you move from target to target – never knowing what eludes you and why there is a seemingly a forward movement but everything still stays the same!

The growth this way is neither sustainable nor satisfactory and whatever output you get as a result would not be worth hiding your true self and pretending as someone else!

B. **Throw that mask away and be yourself** - when you are at your personal best, you accomplish some of the best things in life– and irrespective of the size, impact, or financial rewards, you feel truly satisfied and happy!

The idea is not to stop thinking about the designation, recognition, money and whatever else that you associate with success. On the contrary, you must **want it so badly** that you would be willing to **become the person who deserves all those riches in a sustainable way.**

It would mean you having to challenge and get rid of some of your long-held beliefs.

Shilpa: Someone that I've known for years has forever been at it. He is a very successful, passionate and knowledgeable person, who does some awesome work when he acts as himself.

However, it was painful to see that his mask was so thick that even after getting a senior level promotion last year which he was seeking for 2 years, he was back to complaining and bickering in a very short time.

Almost every conversation with him is filled with what is wrong with other people and the organisation and how things are never going to improve.

Continuing to wear the mask is a **definite long-term failure.** You may make some money in the short term – but the only way you will have sustainable growth and fulfilment including loving every dollar you make, is by being yourself.

In the two scenarios, the first one is the infamous "Rat Race" that we all love to hate- but indulge in day in and day out. We want to get out of it but rarely do. And those who do get out of it often get disillusioned and quit.

You do not have to do that.

You could easily switch gears, if you focus inward and be yourself. It will be hard as hell to start with but we can promise you, it will feel like you fully own every single success that you create, filling you up with confidence like never before.

Focusing on being yourself, while strongly facing that troublesome wind and managing to stand tall, would mean that you are honing your skills at being your personal best.

Each one of us have that unique gift and ability to look at things from a completely different perspective. Hiding it because of being worried about whether this will fit or whether someone else will appreciate it, is akin to killing your genius.

This does need courage – courage to look at yourself in the mirror and deciding what you want for yourself at your work environment.

This will get you back in touch with that young boy or girl, who once had big dreams, ideas and energy to make it all a reality.

Stop wearing a suit and a tie, if it is not who you are!

Workplace Behaviour- That Corporate Politics that you are NOT part of!

"You have to learn the rules of the game and then you have to play them better than anyone else"

- Albert Einstein

The most painful part of any work place is the corporate politics and favouritism. Contrary to what most people think, it is not only bottom rung of a company that suffers from this issue. It gets weirder and more problematic at the top.

In its worst form, it makes amazing people leave the organisation they once loved and served to the best of their abilities.

In a talk with John Pittard, Ex-CIO of Newscorp and a non-executive director of Australian Energy Market Operator, he shared how many of the turnaround points in his career, were driven by not wanting to play the corporate politics.

Corporate politics refers to the inappropriate and intentional act of power to protect one's own interest. This is THE biggest problem in companies; 90% people would love to see this getting resolved.

However, for the very next question, "Do You engage in corporate politics?", a whopping 95% of people answer with a big NO!

Who then engages in this invisible practice?

The 5%?

These same people sometimes, refer to "management", "HR" and "My Peers" as the source of corporate politics.

Anyone but themselves!

This is actually reassuring. It proves that this practice is more of a figment of everyone's imagination and a tactic to handle uncontrollable stuff in a company than real corruption to be removed. The later would make it a really big problem!

Most people would be aghast at this realisation. Surely, you have heard from X talking about Y doing something that Z didn't ask Y to do. Z shared his dislike with X and then X is telling you in confidence.

Hmm. Seems like you and X are engaged in "corporate politics"!

No, our intention is not to catch you off guard. However, we want to rest this idea firmly that there is no invisible beast other than the one you conjure up in your imagination to handle the work stress and those inevitable disagreements.

In other words, corporate politics is a product of how you and I engage with the environment in our workplace. Especially behaviours that we don't agree with.

This book is not about how to play corporate politics or how not to play it. It is about discovering your power so that you are in control of your career and make conscious choice on how you deal with corporate politics from a position of strength and not in a reactive way.

Let us delve into another one of the massive corporate cultural challenges we have seen being repeated in the corner of every office and in every café and elevator exchange.

Workplace Behaviour- Being 'Busy' As A Fashion Statement

"How is it going?": always the same question
"Busy,": always the same lie"

– Elevator Talk!

It's difficult to give up the amusement of listening to elevator conversations. Over the years, we have noticed that "busy," is probably the most natural response to when people ask, "how is it going?".

We're surrounded by busy people everywhere. Whether it is in office, a coffee shop, an elevator, everyone fancies the idea of being busy.

Why is it so rare to hear replies along the lines of "going great", "productive day" or "not the best day..." or anything that means "things are/are not as they are supposed to be and I am comfortable with that."

Not that we are looking for 'unhappy' responses but definitely something that is closer to truth. Being busy is almost considered to be a hygiene factor in most organisations to the extent that if you're not too busy, you aren't doing enough.

Shilpa: When working for a large bank in Australia, a group of us decided that we will stop using the word "busy," as it was not serving us well.

Of the 6 of us who decided it, unfortunately, 4 went back to their older ways as there was a very quick judgement from their colleagues on how productive they were being.

Only 2 of us who were in the same group could manage it well, because our team environment was conducive to that.

It was quite a liberating feeling to be able to speak the truth as it was.

As of this day, I follow the same principle and it is deeply satisfying.

It is due to the invisible influencers in corporate culture, where being busy is considered to be 'doing well' or at the least, 'working hard, will get there eventually'.

Reflect on it in the privacy of your thoughts.

Are there times when you really can't say how productive or content you feel as you don't want to be taken as someone who is NOT working enough/contributing well? Or are there times when you say it just because it helps you fit in?

You might be thinking, "Yes, I have noticed it, but what difference does it make? Is it really that big a deal if people end up pretending a bit at times?"

Consider again.

Our thoughts and words have meanings. Saying anything and NOT meaning it, is self-damaging, forget about how it impacts others for the time being. Every time we let an opportunity for authenticity to slip away, a subtle shift is created in terms of how we relate to work, the people we interact with and just how we generally feel about ourselves.

This shift induces a gradual stress, which becomes a full-blown crisis for those who decide to introspect and becomes an ever-present, unknowable pain for those who have mastered the art of ignorance.

There are no physically drawn lines in real life that people cross to suddenly become dissatisfied, dishonest or disengaged. It takes time and continued contradictory behaviour.

These negative affirmations, small as they might seem, begin to take root in and affect your daily life and accompanying attitude.

One might ask, If I put an end to my personal pattern of repeating this and become more authentic about my responses to "how's it going", what about my work environment? What about the organisation expectations that I'm supposed to be 150% loaded all the time? What about the prospects of people respecting me as the force that I know myself to be?

We would ask you to consider how much of that concern is real and how much of it is perceived?

If you seriously think that you work for an organisation that needs you to be 150% loaded 100% of the time, it is time to switch jobs, because let's face it – you're not going to get your intended objective in an environment like that, no matter how 'okay' or 'great' it's going for you at the moment. There will always be a moving target. Always!

Let's see how the magic of "being authentic" plays out in your own career.

Consider a time when you got promoted. You would recall that you were on top of your game immediately before and more importantly, after the promotion.

You'd remember that when you just got promoted, you did

not have any doubts about how the organisation perceives your contributions. This freedom from being constantly judged and evaluated allowed you to let go of the unnecessary worries and comparisons, resulting in optimal performance. Think about it, you definitely weren't saying you were 'too busy' as commonly at that time!

Wouldn't it be great if we can feel such freedom most of the time?

If you are too busy but do not feel particularly productive, maybe you are satisfying yourself with mindless action without a direction.

If it is true, it will catch up with you. And it will not be nice when it finally does.

Being the real you at your workplace will be far more rewarding than feeling compelled to fake it.

"Your authenticity is your biggest competitive advantage"

– Carla Harris

Let us consider another organisational behaviour that seems to be hurting others but actually creates significantly severe issues for the ones who act in this way.

Workplace Behaviour- Winning at All Costs

"You stop noticing the negativity when you stop looking for it."

There was once a Calvin & Hobbes cartoon where Calvin wonders why people aren't happy.

Hobbes responds, "Are you kidding? Your fingernails are a joke, you've got no fangs, you can't see at night, your pink hides are ridiculous, your reflexes are nil, and you don't even have a tail. Of course, people aren't happy!"

From Hobbes' perspective, as a tiger, nothing could be further from the truth.

Ironically, we act the same way during the vast majority of our discussions, or at least in a work environment where the stakes are much lower than in our personal lives.

Like Hobbes, we bring our 'amazing' power of 'reasoning' and perceived command over 'absolute truth' to most discussions, often without digging deep to establish that 'absolute truth'.

Depending on how senior we are to the person we're speaking to, or how loud we are in a group, or how strongly 'whatever-helps-me-win' attitude we display, we like getting our way without much consideration to what is on the other side of the table.

Why do we do that?

Because we are so habitual of this innate desire to be at the top. We always want to win everything – every argument, every deal, every promotion. Everything!

And in that process, we sideline our own standards and beliefs for that one small win.

Even in your personal life, haven't there been instances when you said that wrong thing to your friends or your partner, one that created a lot of guilt? Just because you were desperate to win that argument?

This desperate urge to win is highly damaging to your corporate environment, your teams and your long-term growth!

The sad thing is that this pattern has become so intrinsic in your behaviour on every scale you can think of. It is visible in the kitchen with your partner, on the phone with a friend, in a meeting with your boss, on the couch at 1 am yelling at a politician on television or simply going crazy about how your favourite team is playing!

The problem emerges when, in accordance to the unfortunately quintessential human nature, we act as if our opinion is the only one which can possibly be right.

Intellectually, most of us are aware that we don't know everything and that we are constantly learning through our interactions with the environment. However, in reality, we act as if our view is the only sane view in the room.

All of us have experienced it at one time or the other. For some this is a daily occurrence at work and usually very frustrating to deal with.

Think of it, why would there be anything wrong with your own opinion? There's no one else you listen to more!

However, given that most of us spend our lives within a small set of like-minded people, with similar challenges, similar lifestyle, similar choices and aptitude, there is a stronger tendency to judge all of our other discussions through the same tinted glasses that we use when we are with this small set of people.

"People in one group/category are often insensitive to or at best unaware of the needs, feelings, rationale of others."

– Shilpa K

There is also a significant role played by corporate culture, performance measurement and the current formal and informal reward systems.

In today's highly competitive world, individuals at all levels within organisations compete for positions, promotions, money, incentives or often just a pat on the back.

This results in an inherent need in people to win at all times, especially when they just know that they're right – which is probably 90% of the time!

The other Hobbes like behaviour is holding on to the information and not sharing openly.

Kapil: Recently one of my clients shared his decision about leaving his company that is going through a lot of leadership changes. While he is very well aligned with the changes, his VP's tendency to keep things close to his heart and not share information is the primary reason for leaving his job.

He shared one such instance of how he was in a meeting with the CEO, where he ended up looking very uninformed, because his manager held on to a critical information about the CEOs earlier meeting with a partner.

While in itself it looks like a lack of foresight and a general mistake on the VPs part, the repetition of this pattern of behaviour throughout last year has been a significant issue to deal with.

The only reason people would ever withhold information is because they are worried about their own little insecurities. In the above example, the VP is so worried about his own job that in a desperate bid to look useful, he is just making his team look bad!

If you are a manager, it is all the more worse, not just because you are damaging others by holding information and making them work in dark, but also because you are becoming a bottleneck and too important to ever grow out of that role!

This is highly prevalent in every single company, whether it is big or small.

Kapil: One of my clients has been facing significant frustration due to his co-founder CEO displaying this behaviour very regularly. The communication with this CEO has become a never-ending discussion about inclusion.

His approach has now shifted from having transactional discussion with this CEO to clearer definition of responsibilities and delegation. This, hopefully will create a shift in accountabilities and bring about the change that is desperately needed to fuel their growth.

Let us now take a look at the usual blockers we have in our life and career and understand the massive impact it has on our ability to actually act towards our dreams.

DEMYSTIFYING THE MYTHS

"What you allow is what will continue"

If someone asked you to walk blindfold, you could do it for fun. You could do it to compete in a game as well but you couldn't do it as an everyday rule in life.

However, that is how we do most things in life.

We have so many limiting beliefs about how life has to be lived and how external environment has to be dealt with.

For the most part, we don't get to really face these demons of our limiting beliefs till we eventually hit a crisis. When that crisis comes, majority of us are able to resolve the challenges because most of us are really good at reacting well to circumstances. Therefore, crisis resolution isn't really a big issue here.

The real issue is not noticing it generally in life, despite being surrounded by these limiting beliefs all the time. The small challenges keep piling up eventually creating the crisis, which most of us solve and go back to living life without awareness, till next one hits.

Let us dwell upon this for a moment.

If you have a spot on the back of your neck, you wouldn't see it until it becomes sore. Even if this spot becomes the biggest reason why you don't get certain outcomes – for instance, being in a situation where people avoid you!

This will then be a way of life – you wouldn't know what you are missing as that is the only way you know the world is.

In this section, we look at the typical mindset that you have developed because of your background, upbringing and experiences in life.

The gut-feel reaction you have in each of those has been proved wrong umpteen number of times but the selective nature of your attention and focus creates a picture that things are fine!

These blockers are often unchallenged and this section will enable you to identify and hopefully get rid of a lot of what you have been unnecessarily holding on to in life, not realising that it is not serving you well.

You Gradually Grow – Anything fast will come down crashing

"It is hard to lose when your standards are low"

95% of us grew in middle class. Middle class is a safe haven for people. It is the norm for the world.

However, a large number of us look at ways by which we can make it to the top of the pecking order.

For financial growth, almost everyone follows the same old pattern. You work your butt off, you put money in property, you buy some shares. If you are a bit more enterprising, you get in a group together with friends to buy a bigger property.

Next level of "enterprising" folks invests in Amazon or friend's or family's business. Or consider creating an application for some under serviced market!

Take a step back – why don't most people take bigger risks, get bigger rewards? We don't mean to say that you ought to consider going to a casino and risk it all!

Now think about it – you are more likely to success, if you can keep an eye on the emerging trends in an area that you have capability in and interest to serve. However, even when you know this fact fully, you don't do that.

Because of the middle-class belief that gradual growth is a good thing. Anything that grows fast must either be illegal, or plain luck.

Steve Jobs made 1M in 1978 – guess how much he was worth in 1980? 250M!

Jane Lu, the founder of Showpo grew at 300% month on month after initial hiccups and massive failures. Her wealth shot straight out to $116M worth in 5 years.

It is not just about being rich, it actually about who you become in that process, in pursuing that dream and impacts everything in your life- relationships, health, achievements. Everything!

Kapil: the story of my weight loss

For a majority of my adult life, I was overweight by about 20 KG. As a 172 cm tall guy (5 ft 8 in), I weighed about 86 KG. I hated it. I wanted to change it but I loved my food too much.

Then I got to know about the 7-day GM diet – where you eat different stuff every day. Lost 8 KG in 7 days. I was on top of the world!

My parents and other well-wishers said that, everything sustainable has to be gradual and this isn't good for you and it will not work.

They were right. I gained that 8 KG right back within 1-2 months.

Despite being married to a health buff, I just didn't get this part of my life in control and this kind of a thing continued for 18 years- on and off.

I knew it was simple- food and exercise.

Simple. I also really wanted to do it!

But anything that I had to do over a long stretch of time was the big blocker – as the only way to do it was to **do it slowly and gradually.**

Or so I thought at the time!

Till 2017, gym for me was for those other people who are way too conscious of their physique. "I am not crazy like them" was how I thought. However, I longed to have a stronger, leaner body.

Weight reduction till then was a matter of doing a "7 days diet" or a new year resolution or something worse! I did try a lot of different things, but all resolutions disappeared the moment I saw something really tasty!

A friend used to mock, "if you put something in front of him, he thinks the world would end unless he eats it!!" And then there were those social occasions – one too many of them, when you would eat just to make a point of proving to someone that you don't really care – I mean, how foolish was that!!

I recall trying "positive thinking" about my looks, only to find it disappear when I walked past a window!

In other words, Bad, Bad, bad! It felt terrible – like a loss, like an inability, something I can never do. Too big a target to take on, as I will definitely fail – everyone I knew failed in this effort! "It is impossible to not eat that yummy cake or pudding!"

Maybe you too are getting Been-there-done-that feeling?

The motivation – decision to change

And I said to my body, softly, "I want to be your friend."
It took a long breath and replied, "I've been waiting my whole life
for this."

– Nayyirah Waheed

It changed in 2017. It was not a gradual change that took place over the years or that I took the plunge after years of frustration. Nope! It wasn't like that. It was in making for years but otherwise was an overnight change! It was a simple change of belief about myself and how I saw myself.

This change of how I viewed myself, took one sleepless night and one change.

Long story short (interested readers can read the story in my linked in article related to it), I lost 16 KG in 16 weeks without a single cheat day, without any temptations or setbacks or brave-heart efforts.

The "Everyone I knew failed in this!" disappeared in thin air.

The "Only sustainable thing is what works with most people", was never going to come back to my life.

This was replaced by "I can do anything that I put my mind on to".

I didn't make any hard choices or sacrifices. This is where most diets fail. In fact, this is where most change fail.

You fight hard against an old desire, an old way of doing things – or you overthink and over analyse it. Knowing your target, developing new ways of doing it and executing without any cheat days or cheat times. That is all it takes.

The 10X rule by Grant Cardone sums it up very well. When you want to do something and you are really committed about it – you get obsessed with that and it just becomes the most important thing in your mind. You then think really big and solve really big problems.

It took me 16 weeks to reduce 16 KG – just too damn perfect – as I had written down. I don't believe it was a coincidence. It has been 2 years. My food habits have changed, my health is on an upward trajectory, my friends and family have become healthier and the change in my psychology and attitude about *what I can do, when I put my mind on to something*, is just a great beginning.

Saying it to yourself – "Someday I will get it" isn't great but is still better than "I cannot grow any faster". The latter is damaging you in ways you don't realise.

Believe that it is possible for people to grow disproportionately and it doesn't need manipulation.

Give yourself a chance to be awesome!"

Work Hard and You Will Get There

"Your growth is directly proportional to your self-belief"

Hard work is essential for success but you have to work hard at things that will give you outcomes you want. The biggest question, you have to ask is, **Work Hard at WHAT?**

What is the direction you are going towards? What are you focused on? What does **hard work** mean for you?

Few years back, we decided to do a DYI project of building a deck in our backyard. We decided to build it over an 8X4 meter area- dividing it in two levels, with a 10-inch step in between.

The 4X4 meter area for Level 1 took us 2 days (8 hours) to build. The other 4X4 meter area for Level 2, was 10 inches higher and it took us 1 month of evening work – (about 100 hours)!

The reason for this productivity loss was that for us; **momentum became more important than reflection and planning.**

We built the base of entire Level 2 with over 100+ bricks supporting the base. In addition, the time to put base frame and horizontal alignment, mistakes, tearing it up and re-doing some parts- took 100 hours!!

Despite the truth facing us right in the face, we never actually questioned it DURING the process that why this was taking inordinate amount of time!

It was only after a friend got his entire similar sized deck done in a matter of a week, it occurred to us to question!

We found that if only we had taken a few hours or maybe less in planning, some more YouTube videos, we would have taken completely different approach of creating the base for the second part of the deck!

Some of the readers may even laugh at us – but reflecting back – hasn't there been a time in your life when you have worked hard because "I don't want to lose momentum" only to have something completed in 10 times more effort than otherwise?

Each one of us had those moments.

And no, you cannot hide these kinds of moments behind "it was a good learning experience".

It was a wasted experience. It was mindless movement and fallacy of forward motion feeling like progression, each one of us get into!

We tend to believe that hard work is a solution to most problems.

Work hard. Work VERY hard, by all means, with everything you got – but more importantly DEFINE, what are you going to work hard at. Make a conscious choice, what you will NOT be doing.

A donkey works hard at one single thing. Most people work hard at a few things- working hard doesn't produce results.

In corporate life, too many people just say – "I work so hard but my work is not rewarded".

You could work hard all your life pushing a car sitting inside but it won't move.

Consider your past success – did it come from working hard or did it come from having a direction and THEN working hard on it?

"Results Come from Laser Focused Efforts"

A Laser beam has comparatively low energy but it is so focused that it can pierce steel. Your focus is the key to the vault, where your success is waiting.

Let us consider another thing that most people will intellectually not agree with but people still operate with that blocker being a part of their everyday reality.

Those Are Extraordinary Individuals

"Opportunity is missed by most because it is dressed in overalls and looks like work"

– Thomas Edison

How many of you had the thought, "some people are just more talented!"? While this may have pushed you to try harder at times, weren't there times when it also gave you a ticket to look at your perceived limitations in the eye and say, "I wasn't actually born to do it"?

And didn't it give you reasons to give up on the possibilities and the dreams that you had?

This belief in talent is a major hurdle to what we can accomplish. It is a "No Entry" sign erected by us, in our own path, towards the objective that we want to achieve but can't get past the sign.

When you know that you do not have the necessary talent to do something, you detach yourself from your path, consequently failing to achieve the things that you truly want.

Most people think that Bill Gates, Warren Buffett, Steve Jobs, Richard Branson and other business moguls are prodigies and that there is no way for anyone to catch up to them or do what they have done.

This idea of someone being extraordinary is just an excuse people give, so that they can be satisfied that this kind achievement is beyond their capability. It gives them a permission to be average.

The truth, however is completely different. Each of them started at ground zero. Each of them had multitude of failures.

Each thought a million times that they may have to give up but they relentlessly pursued their passion.

Brandon Dawson, a successful entrepreneur, currently a partner of Grant Cardone, was rejected 120 times in trying to raise US$1M capital. Even Walt Disney was laughed out by 3 major banks for his US$17M Loan.

Everyone starts somewhere. Everyone fails- not once, not twice but many, many times. Those who keep getting up in a relentless pursuit of their dreams, get to see the victory.

If you talk to ANY self-made millionaire or billionaire – they will laugh at the idea that they are unique, brilliant or lucky.

They are different – that is true.

When you see a multi-millionaire – you first have an awe – and when you have spent a couple of hours in his or her company, you realise their accomplishments are a result of doing small things consistently.

"Ordinary Things Consistently Done Produce Extraordinary Results"

– Keith Cunninghum

While there are often genetic factors that contribute to the fact that someone is good at something, such as a great memory, or someone with developed arms - like Michael Phelps, perhaps, but most vocations do not require a brain that can calculate faster than a calculator or be a "genius" that is a necessity to be outstanding in that area.

However, most people take a look at those outstanding geniuses and then generalise it as something that is a MUST HAVE talent at the base of it.

Take any elite performer and read about how they have come to this level and how they nurtured their passion, and you will find that their hard work & focus was the key to their success - not luck or innate talent.

Shilpa: For a long time, I considered my intuitive abilities to be the primary reason for my success. Hard as it was to break that pattern, I've come to recognise that my intuition is actually one of the many outcomes of my hard work over the years and a pattern I had come to recognize without conscious choices.

You may have similar challenges and breaking those patterns will remove any ideas about "people, who achieve greatness are aliens".

The first step is to recognise that **it was the effort** you put in all along.

Write down your successes on a piece of paper and consider your environment, the accompanying challenges, and how you overcame those. You probably had a reliable support system, which you worked hard to create, as well.

At the end, there will be enough reasons to give yourself a pat on the back for all the hard work that you had put in.

Next time when you feel di-spirited because you're not inherently good at something, remember that nothing comes naturally. A lot of those skills you will develop along the way, as you pursue and **walk the path** that gets you there.

The idea is to develop new patterns, where focus is on the small wins, ongoing forward movement, and putting in the necessary effort towards achieving these short-term objectives as the key to success.

It is now time to look at your heroes afresh and appreciate that every single one of these individuals worked very hard to get to where they are. The same is possible for you.

Another significant delusion people have about the those, who have achieved extraordinary results is that **You can't have both Happiness and Richness at the same time.**

Growing up in the middle-class world, we somehow get this idea that people who are rich are actually unhappy or have so many problems that it is not worth being rich. This view gets further enhanced by the news and movies that glorifies the issues that some of those rich people have and the idea that richness and happiness don't go together, get cemented.

It almost feels like, one of the favourite pastimes in the middle class is to talk about how successful people are unhappy and how our own life is fantastic under this cosy little roof.

This is delusional. How many rich and successful people you personally know whose life is bad? Knowing them through media is not the same thing.

Discard all those childhood comics, mythology portrayals of poor dude and rich villain and all other stories that you have been tuned to absorb.

Let us also consider the needs of every human being. Each person in this world wants 3 things above everything else – Love, Connection and Fulfillment. Without these three, nothing you can get is worth it.

What makes people think that the rich and successful will not go after these same needs? Is it because they have more money or they do not value them or they want to run away from love and connection?

"Wealth creates the ability to fully experience life"

– Henry David Thoreau

Each individual has the ability to be very successful and actually generate significant amount of wealth, only if they let go of this one belief that being rich will make them sad and lonely.

The fact is that money is not evil – SOME people make bad use of it. But MOST people treat it with respect. If someone gives you a $20 note, you trust it to be worth $20.

Money is trust. It is the pursuance of money at all cost to our life, or of our dear ones that is stupid. If you make money by creating value – it is a great thing to have.

Go ahead and do what you need to do to get really rich. You CAN have your cake and eat it too.

WHY PEOPLE DO NOT TAKE ACTIONS

"The secret of change is to focus all your energy not on fighting the old, but on building the new."

– Dan Millman

Now that we know, there are some blockers we have about the world that we operate in and how we view success, it is time to look at our internal battles that we constantly get into – in our heads.

One of our friends has forever been a planner. He has a plan to do a major renovation at home for 6 years, a plan to open a business for 8 years and is now harbouring a plan for impacting the children in Australia by providing life-education system built on a similar model as other highly immersive programs. He has many more fantastic ideas, some of which we don't even know of.

He isn't different from most people. He is extremely intelligent, highly successful and an amazing idea man. You too probably know someone like that. Such people get really motivated thinking about these big ideas.

However, a majority of them do nothing with these ideas. Their focus is not on the small things. Their eyes are set at high level and taking any action in that direction in a sustainable way is a significant challenge for them.

What is up with them? Why don't they take actions even when they intellectually know that without actions, nothing they think of or talk about it worthwhile?

Let us consider some of the prevalent reasons why people stop in their tracks despite knowing how to do what.

My Situation is Unique

"What sets you apart can sometimes feel like a burden and it's not. And a lot of the time, it's what makes you great."

– Emma Stone

Kapil: I had my biggest crisis time in 2012 when I lost a senior level promotion due to reasons that were not of my making. These reasons were "reasonable" but I was so deep in the forest that the only thing I saw was the trees around me.

My sense of entitlement made me extremely negative and I started demonstrating massively destructive behaviour.

Fortunately, instead of firing me, the company engaged a coach as a last resort (I didn't know it then!). The coach, Arthur Walmsley flew from Melbourne to spend an entire day with me.

The first 3 hours must have been a pain for him and he must have thought of shouting at me with all his might, but somehow controlled it!

He did break my barriers when he finally pulled me up and made me see the impact by literally telling me that if he was my manager, he would have fired me on the spot! (his words were much harsher than that and hit harder – but I needed it then)

Once I calmed down, he told me how he had met Shilpa that morning for breakfast, which surprised me a lot. He had told her not to share and because she was deeply concerned about me, she didn't. It was a bigger surprise for me to know that I was being a jerk at home as well.

Me, the man who always put family first, the great husband and father – was being a jerk!

Then he made me realise, how I was continuously letting my manager, Paul Whybrow, down, a man who I respected immensely (and didn't blame at all for my situation – I blamed HIS manager! I had to blame someone to make me feel right!!)

After that, things changed- I got that coveted promotion next year and it was nothing compared to the valuable lessons I got from Arthur. Those lessons stay with me till date!

One, I recognised that **how we show up at one place, we show up at all the places.** We can fool ourselves to think that we can be calm and poised– and probably for a few hours, it is possible – but in a very short time, people around us can sense that things are not right.

Two, I found out how it is **possible to change VERY FAST** – if only we create a leverage on ourselves by converting **our "should" into a "MUST"** (as Tony Robbins says), allow ourselves to be open and challenge our current set of beliefs and actions.

Three, the power of leveraging others – just by allowing someone experienced, with a view of the forest instead of the trees you see, to have a look in your life. This kept getting validated as I coach people across the globe, who in just 2-3 discussions, say that they are completely surprised that this kind of a change is possible in such a short time.

And Four, I recognised that my situation wasn't as unique as I thought it was. It was only after meeting with people and helping them change their lives, I see that this is so ingrained in our society!

Each of us have been guilty of saying this at one point of time or other;

"If only you knew, what I have gone through"

"Most people would give up long before they get to where I am now"

"There is no way, you can even understand what I am facing or what I faced"

Your situation is NOT unique. There are 3.3 billion or more working people in the world. There are millions in your own city and thousands in your community and immediate vicinity.

What you are going through, someone else has gone through. And may be much more. And that someone has found a solution to his/her problem.

You are never too old to take that step, to go to that university, to do that masters/PhD course or change your job. It doesn't really matter even if you are 70-years-old. Based on your tons of experience, you may have a huge craving for learning and possibilities of a significant growth.

A few years back, our 53 years' old neighbour in Sydney left his 30 years job at Cisco in a senior position and started doing masters. In 2018, he started pursuing his PhD!

Shilpa: I knew someone at Westpac, who was in his late 50s and decided to get into a medical school. It surprised me a lot at the time because I was still new to Australia and didn't realise that the rules I had grown up with, didn't actually apply everywhere!

You are also not too young!

Jack Bloomfield, at the age of 16, is an Australian entrepreneur in online business, giving talks across Australia and is also attending school, while making millions in his business.

Jane Lu of Showpo could have led an average life working in her job but had a spark of creativity and persistence to become a $100M+ worth individual in a short period of 5 years.

> *Kapil:* I once knew someone in Microsoft, who at 27 year of age was a Director of Technology and his approach, focus and what he brought to table in every single meeting was nothing short of amazing.

"But these people are far and few"

You are right. You will never be that person unless you sit up and decide not to give wind to this age issue!

Many professionals working for different size organisations, especially those who have been working for 5+ years get deeply concerned about what they know and what they have done – will not be useful outside.

> *Kapil:* When I decided to get into coaching, I was really worried about my credibility in this area. There were even considerations of going to a university and spend 2 precious years!
>
> My coach made me write down 25 credibility statements about myself and see how it is related to the coaching industry.
>
> It was an eye opener! Each point had some relevance! Even before I got fully into coaching, I had immense credibility which I carried from the corporate world.

What you have done so far has built up some credibility. While credibility is about other people believing what you say you are, at first it is about **you having the belief that you are credible.**

So – if you have any doubt about your confidence and credibility – we challenge you to write 25 statements – and then relate it to what you want in life – you would get a FIRE inside you!!

What you are, what you have done is always valuable – you have done it yourself and there is always a parallel in the new industry you want to go in.

The other side of the coin is changing too many jobs and finding yourself facing this "no one will give me a job since I haven't shown loyalty towards any company". True, it will be a concern but **it is not a show stopper.**

Don't become slave of the "situation". Focus on the "Uniqueness"

Shilpa: In 1999, during the Kargil war, a 24-year-old young captain from Indian Army, Major DP Singh, lost his right leg in a mortar shell attack. I interviewed him for my video podcast "Version 2.0 and Beyond" in June 2019, where he shared some of the previously unspoken aspects of his story (it can be searched on YouTube and searching for "Major DP Singh Shilpa Kulshrestha")

As we got down to the more human aspects of his life, he shared that even before he was taken to the operation table to amputate his leg, he had started framing his thoughts about the speed with which he needed to move forward, despite the challenges in front of him.

Each one of us have insurmountable challenges. What we do with that adversity and to what extent do we push ourselves to win it over, defines how far will we go in the long run.

Major DP Singh decided to make long distance running as his life goal as this seemed to be the biggest challenge, he could put himself to, despite the fact that he was never fond of it in his past life – when he had both legs.

He wanted to prove to himself that he can do anything in this world. It took him more than a decade to make things work and rise above and beyond all odds.

Today with an amputated right leg, partial hearing loss of both ears, partial removal of intestine and 50 shrapnel still embedded in his body, Major D P Singh is the first blade runner of India, first amputee skydiver and a motivational speaker adored by millions.

He says that his accident was the best thing that could have happened to him and he would not have it any other way.

It may look like a very humble statement but he says this with absolute clarity and realism. If he hadn't got injured, he would have been just like millions of other people who serve their nation to the best of their abilities.

However, he wouldn't have been the person, whose name people across the world would wear on their t-shirts.

His differentiation and uniqueness came from his ability to see past his limitations and constraints and focus on accepting the situation as it is and then going ahead with everything and playing it full.

"Accept the situation that you are in. And then go ahead with all that you have".

– Major DP Singh

What is your excuse?

Kapil: When I finally decided that I did not belong in my job, I went through another crisis in life – my partner asked me to apply to other companies but despite having a senior leadership role in a large fortune 200 organisation, I was just very reluctant!

Initially I thought, it is my loyalty to this company, then I thought there is something wrong with the company environment and looked for those reasons, then I switched to "everyone will expect me to do the same thing".

I even said,

"I don't want to make money as that is the cause of all the problems!" as if money somehow drove me to do evil things!!

"My time for growth is done, it is my kids time!" as if it was mutually exclusive!

"I need to focus on higher purpose of being calm and satisfied with what I have" as if I was driven by the lust of accomplishing things at the cost of my soul!!

Looking back, I realise how stupid each of those things was!

From one boat to other, I kept jumping around the block never realising that the whole time, the biggest thought I had was, I have been here with this company too long, which has made me a bit rusty and there is no value for my abilities outside.

Working with my coach Graham Heath, I got rid of these, I discovered my direction and made a call to become a coach. In fact, Graham said that in his decades of coaching, he has suggested it to only a handful of people.

That created a significant confidence and following his lead, I was able to see a pattern in my life.

Too many of us stay in our head and decide how a conversation is going to turn out, how a deal will turn and "what they will say, if I said what I want to really say". As a result, we don't even open our mouth.

When we coach people, everyone starts with the premise that their situation is very unique and there is no one in the entire world who would have gone through what they are going through.

If you are thinking, "wait a second, this doesn't make sense" – we agree! It doesn't!

Because it is NOT true!

Being able to get it out of our head is often the start of sharing with others, leveraging others and becoming powerful in our life.

In our 4 weeks transformation challenge program GEED (Get Excited Every Day), we work with an exclusive group of 20 people across 4 weeks and across the globe to start their transformation journey. Within the first 5 days, about 60% people are surprised about what they find out about themselves and within the first 10 days, we have 80% people sharing how something they held on to is gone forever and has transformed their life. More information can be found at https://scintillate.com.au/break-new-grounds/

Fact is, more often than not, we are too busy looking down at our expenses, our limitations, our situations, our constraints that we never look up. If you work to discover what is important to you, you will look down only 5% time at those other things.

Imagine what that shift of 95% focus to your dreams will do to your life!

When we quit our respective jobs, our family and friends were shell shocked with the income dip that we were getting into – literally 75% drop.

It soon paid off – as you see the amount of impact we are causing. It paid off in ways that is financially satisfying but beyond that is spiritually fulfilling!

There is Never a better time than right now to do awesome things.

Let the Stars Align

You know that it will NEVER be perfect. There will always be that one more thing to do, that final tweak, after which you believe that you will be done.

The Stars will NEVER Align

Kapil: A number of years back, I was flying to UK for a client presentation, along with my manager, his manager and some other people flying from US. I even remember seeing the Indian movie star Amir Khan at the Hyderabad airport on a wheelchair, on my way to London. This was back when he was injured shooting for the movie "Gajni".

I worked on the presentation throughout the flight and got it to almost perfection, with a few missing pieces. I knew I will be able to fill in those pieces with my business head Shankar Srinivasan (in a different flight than me) when we reach London as we had good 3 hours gap between flight landing and our presentation.

As it happens, my flight was delayed and it was barely touch and go for us. As the cab rushed to the client office, about 45 min drive away, I was huddled with Shankar in the backseat of the cab, going through the slides.

He cut down the 25 slides to a bare 10, And he even removed all the content from one of the slides, keeping only the heading there, adding "Discussion" in front of it.

It was tumultuous and extremely painful to see the beauty of it getting destroyed in 20 min!

We made it in the meeting and won the multi-million-dollar deal.

And I learnt a huge lesson that day!

"Perfection is an excuse to mediocrity"

Most people keep trying to get it right and right and right till it lands up in the bin!

You have been there and done that. Right?

The presentation that had amazing graphics, fantastic animation and really was a piece of art but when you presented to client, it couldn't go past 2 slides before it was ripped to pieces!

The code you cut, that compiles in a single go – yet has a thousand bugs!

The perfect CV you made, that was rejected by hundreds of companies and recruiters!

The perfect document you wrote, requirements, functional specs, test cases, project plans that just took hell of a time and didn't get ANY reviews from anyone!

Kapil: A client once made a web application that was to revolutionise the security industry – only it never took off as he kept perfecting it till eternity. As he narrated this story, the only thing he could say about that was, "it was an idea before its time".

As if things have a magical time associated with their implementation and adoption. It almost seems like, having an idea of having a warp engine that will allow interstellar travel but the idea is before its time!!

Shilpa: I remember when I was doing my Chartered Accountancy, I would spend so much time perfecting my answers to some questions that I would end up leaving no time for the remaining questions. As a result, I would always end up missing questions worth 35-40 marks.

Think about it. Had I attempted the full paper; I had the potential of getting marks in 90s or even 100. But with my perfect answers there was no way, I could have got more than 65.

My quest of perfection wasn't an anomaly that I alone engaged in.

The countless hours you spent preparing something that never quite got there and when it did, someone ended up criticizing it, causing it to go nowhere. You have been there.

Waiting for the stars to align before we consider something completed or start something new is about this penchant of perfection that we all have to a different degree! The reality is, perfection creates mediocrity and not beauty as it is intended.

Why? Because things don't get done! And what is not "done" is pretty much wastage.

Even when it gets done, it brings in criticism and unexpected negative feedback!

What you want to do has to be done with a core goal of accomplishing an objective FIRST. Then it becomes about how much right you can get it. Get it as right as your target audience likes.

Then, keep evolving it to get more people to adopt it.

This book is a live example of that. Surely there are grammatical errors, many sentences are long – but we would rather get it out to people to help them start gaining from it than keep it to ourselves for years, in pursuit of perfection.

Shilpa: I once met someone in a party who took pride in the fact that he was writing a book that was going to "change the world" and he would be ever remembered for leaving this legacy. I tried a lot to get him out of that mindset but nothing happened.

As you probably guessed, he was writing that book for years! And you too know, he will never finish.

Even if he does, it would not probably turn out the way he wants because we all know how a perfectionist works.

If you feel terrible about your own perfection or lack of action – it may bring some comfort to know that even Newton got into seclusion and continued his work in desperation for fear of critique from the members of Royal Society.

Perfection makes it extremely difficult to see how much return you are getting on your investment of time. Chasing perfection is a waste of absolutely useful time and opportunity. Things that you want to do well, will still not get done to perfection, even if you keep working on them forever.

Kapil: I once made a mistake of challenging a tester that he cannot find a bug in my code. He found 20+ in one day.

With my ego bruised, I worked day and night to get it perfect and he still found serious bugs.

The cycle continued at least 4-5 times before I got it right. Took 2 weeks to get this right and 16 hours days.

Next time, I partnered with him and we did similar sized program in 2-3 days!

"If it is to be done, it is worth being done well" was misconstrued to "… being done perfectly".

What you want to do will never complete unless you adopt the 80-20 principle. Do 20%, get some runs on the board, collaborate and let your audience/users give feedback to do the remaining 80%.

It Is Probably Not the Right Time

This is a big opportunity buster.

Don't get us wrong – if this is preceded by significant clarity and alignment, it is the right thing to do. However, this is often an excuse to procrastinate or not do something due to ignorance and not well thought through argument.

One of the amazing concepts by Tony Robbins deals with how human beings are driven by 2 fundamental forces: **Fear of Pain and Possibilities of Pleasure.**

If you can spend X amount of time in making $25,000 or in NOT losing $25,000 that you already have, what would you most likely do?

Most people will focus on NOT losing.

That is why it hurts much more when you are cheated of your $10 than when you miss an opportunity to make $100!

If you are caught in an earth quake and see two people. One of them says, "Here, it is good here" and another one shouts, "no, not there, it is dangerous", you are more likely to listen to the second person.

Our hind brain's main function is to keep us safe from any possibility of pain. It is not just psychologically true but also physically. Our entire nervous system evolved to ensure body corrects pain anywhere by sending appropriate signals. Every part of our body has those pain receptors!

Playing it safe is built into our psyche!

Kapil: When I was in year 1 of Engineering, I got 49 percent marks in Maths. This was a big shocker. Maths was my thing. Before that I had never had less than 99.

There was a problem with the exam. There always is! Right? Problem with an external factor.

Well, as it happened, there was indeed a problem with the exam and those who applied for a correction, got a re-exam.

My roommate criticized me heavily when I was applying as it meant taking unnecessary pain! "You have to let go" he said!

But for me, the pain of living with those marks was way too much and that made me act to create a possibility. I jumped on the opportunity. In fact, majority of my friends laughed at me for being "so attached to the past".

I took the exam and got 97 marks. Really shot my % for that year up.

It is not about risk taking, being adaptable or any such behavioural traits. It is about how you associate the pain or reward for an action. We are all significantly more likely to do something to avoid the pain than for maximise the opportunity for pleasure.

"What is wrong with that", you may say, "I may miss on a few opportunities but it keeps things simple".

It is not just missing a few opportunities – it is not even letting a door open that was about to swing open, if only you had not stopped it. Imagine how much hidden treasure was lost because of that one single action.

Once you are aware of a potentially good thing – unless there are specific reasons to not do it and not some vague ideas about stars aligning or being 100% right (The Perfection Trap), the question we ought to ask is not "Why" but "Why Not".

Those who are in the habit of living in a circle- get up, go to work, come back, spend time with family, TV, sleep, get up... and on and on – would definitely be under the delusion of forward movement. Indeed, there is forward movement for even such people as somehow, somewhere, some learning happens and they do move forward.

But at a snail's pace.

We know that you are not someone who is happy moving at a snail's pace. We can tell. Because you are reading THIS book about fast tracking your career.

And by now, you have an idea that it is not just about fast tracking your career but fast tracking your LIFE and let the career benefit!

We are sure that in your life, there are many such circular motions and slow progress. However, if you look back, there have also been times of huge leaps forward.

Unfortunately, for most of us, those leaps were more of an exception than a rule. What is worse is that you settle down to think that this is the way life is meant to be and that's where you get caught in a mediocre mindset!

"You Will Go Far, Only If You Start Walking"

I Know It All

Kapil: A few months back, an old friend of mine, who is very successful in terms of his achievements and relationships, was here in Sydney. We went for a long walk with a level 2 difficulty. Now Level 2 has some stairs but is mostly smooth terrain.

As we walked – we were talking about health and he was really switched on and kept talking about how he walks 5 km every day, keeping a close eye on his health. All good except, he had a really big pot belly. And he was huffing and puffing away to glory.

Now, I am a coach, I tell it as it is – it was a bit of a struggle for him to accept that he had a massive challenge.

Once we broke down that barrier – he opened up about how despite his massive financial accomplishments, he is really stuck in his career.

Recently, he has been in touch and is now deeply engaged with me on his career transformation to help take it to a completely new level.

Shilpa: When the world famous Sadguru came to Australia, many of my friends went to see him. I remember sitting with them a day before the event, when a friend remarked, how she already knew everything that he was about to talk about.

It didn't go down well for me when I couldn't stop myself from saying, "and what do you do with all that fantastic knowledge?"!

Most people consider that they know everything. Many of them actually do know a lot of stuff but they just do not do anything with that knowledge.

What adds to their damage is motivational videos. Such videos have many good thoughts rotating around a core message.

Unfortunately, the way our brain works is, by finding any familiar point in whatever we absorb and latching on to it as a safety mechanism.

In a motivational video, we tend to get aligned with that one thought that is in the periphery and is aligned with how we already think.

This then defies the whole purpose of that motivational video, which instead of helping us challenge ourselves, makes us feel good about us already knowing "it".

Either you can use an external stimulus to challenge yourself, or just to validate your thinking.

Those who progress, use it to challenge themselves and then build on it- they CHANGE something in their life. They ACT.

> *"You progress ONLY when you ACT"*
>
> **- Shilpa K**

In the early part of our journey as Mindset Transformation Coaches, this troubled us massively. The "I-Know-It-All" seemed so prevalent that it felt almost like a disease eating away the society.

This is an entry barrier for most people. It is because of the safety mechanism built in our hind brain- "Is there a danger?". This safely mechanism acts like a filter for most people to not let in anything that challenges their current perspective easily.

There is no way past it unless we make a conscious choice to challenge it. What hurts most people is their automatic response to most things that happen in their environment.

Shilpa: This was quite well expressed in a thought experiment by Ron Malhotra, a Melbourne based wealth strategist, on the set of my podcast "Version 2.0 and Beyond". Assume that you are on level 34 of a tall building and someone is on level 10. Assume you are both looking in the same direction and you call this person to come up and see that awesome view from your floor.

She responds that her view is awesome too. As you keep telling about various facets, she tries to comprehend it **based on her current parameters.**

You get more and more puzzled as she continues to ask you about **what is different for you**, as both of you are looking in the same direction, at the same thing.

Eventually you realise that it is not possible to describe that experience unless she experiences it herself.

Most people want to know the experience without actually making effort to, well experience it!

Shilpa: When we went for the medical test for our PR in Australia, we found out for the first time that our 8 year' old daughter actually had an acute far sight problem.

Later in the week, when she got her glasses, she herself was very surprised that the world looked completely different from how it was earlier.

There was no reference point for her to compare it against!

Our current set of reality, surroundings, constraints and beliefs end up defining how we interpret something. To go beyond – to a mythical level 34, you need a completely new set of eyes and guidance.

You have to see to believe.

The "I-Know-It-All" just kills YOUR own possibilities.

Kapil: One of my mentees shared a story about how he met with a buyer agent and made a decision on the spot about leveraging his services.

Once he bought it, he told the agent that a month back, he wouldn't have considered meeting him, let alone buying anything on the spot.

What changed for him in that month was the coaching program that he was part of and the value he had seen of trusting the universe, environment and people.

Getting out of "I-Know-It-All" attitude, opens up a whole new world of possibilities.

Just knowing something is not enough – if you want the knowledge to be your best friend and create the results you want, you have to really know it, feel it and most of all, act on it.

The Cost Is Too Much for Now

A fellow coach from India shared a story sometimes back. He has a client who was leading a $10M business in India. This client's business wasn't scaling up well and, on his advice, engaged an operational consultant to give him a proposal.

This consultant shared a proposal that at the cost of ~$16,000 per year, he can take care of all his operational needs with benefits neatly laid out in the proposal.

This coach advised the client to take the deal but the client was very reluctant as he thought he knew his business well.

Finally, after a continued dialogue for a few weeks, the client took that deal.

In flat 3 months, his business started growing by leaps and bounds – growing as much as 20% per month!

All because his time became free to focus on things that really mattered!

One little change gave him an ROI of 100X!

As you hear this story, you would absolutely agree that it made a lot of sense for that client to invest on this. However, this isn't without irony. It always looks easy AFTER the fact.

This may look like an example, where there was one obvious course of action. However, most of us live our life like that.

We want evidences of *"will this work for me?"*, before actually experiencing it ourselves. We spend so much time doubting things that we lose the opportunity.

Why do you think that the people who are ready to jump on to opportunities and explore new things, go much ahead in life?

Remember that Maths problem in your school days, that looked impossible to solve, but once you saw the solution, you wonder "why didn't I ever think of it – it was so easy".

In most cases, the solution is trivial but walking that path is the deal!

In our experience as Mindset Transformation Coaches, it is sad to see most people get caught up in this thinking, not taking action and when we look at their life in 1, 2 or 5 years, they have the same life as they had years back. No progress, no growth.

No wonder, so many people end up saying,

I wish, I had…

If only I had…

If I knew then…

There is hardly any way to measure the ROI on your investment on yourself.

But what about the cost of inaction?

What about the cost of all those times, when short term stuff – a car, a house, a watch or something that has a fleeting value became more important than you chasing your dreams and giving it your all?

Kapil: When I was unhappy with my corporate job and discovered a pattern, I knew I had to change into a career where my passion will be my core earning mechanism. I told this to my mentor that when my wife reaches $50K more, I will quit.

He warned me that it is unlikely to happen as my needs and expenses would have increased by then. I didn't listen to him.

He was right. My wife reached $50K more in 3 years and I moved up by a higher amount. But unfortunately, so did our lifestyle, mortgages and other expenses.

The life I am living today was possible much earlier if only I had the courage to see the truth. If only I had considered the opportunity cost. There is no one else I can blame but myself!

"If only I had...."

We are sure that you can draw parallels in your life as well. You too allow those challenges to drive a lot of your decisions. Yet, you have a phone that costs almost $700-$1,000. You drive a great car and you live in a nice house.

You are spending everywhere except on things that will help you grow beyond your current means in ways, currently unimaginable!

Is the solution then to take a leap of faith? Maybe.

Maybe it is to expose yourself to things that you have previously considered impossible.

"Energy Flows Where Focus Goes"

– Tony Robbins

What you focus on becomes BIGGER.

If you focus on possible dangers, side effects, etc. – you will seem bigger and you will get stuck there. If you focus on your limitations/ shortcomings, you will see them more and more.

> We bought our first apartment in 2003 in India for $42,000. The building owner we bought it from, suggested that we should buy in a bigger gated community that he was building about 2 KM away – almost in front of the new IT commercial hub in Hyderabad, India.
>
> The problem was it was about 50% more of the price we were paying for this one. If we had considered getting out of our comfort zone, we could have managed it. We ended up focusing on all that could go wrong by stretching ourselves and bought that smaller apartment.

We sold it in 3 years in about $100K and made good money. That place which we had refused however was selling at $220K.

Calculate it – from 42K to 100K vs 63K to 220K!

When you are too much concerned about the current issues, current challenges, current limitations – you get stuck in the "current" and have smaller gains.

The $ figure here is just symbolic. What we want to focus on is the small game that we end up playing in life because we focus on issues and challenges instead of opportunities.

"There is a difference between being mindful of your constraints and being driven by your constraints"

– Shilpa K

The second one is a sure shot way to a mediocre life.

Kapil: In 2009, the company I worked for, made an investment of sending me here just after the GFC to grow the business substantially.

If they were driven by the external constraints, they would have never done it. They made a measured decision based on the future. They were mindful of the constraints and so I didn't move here till we had signed the deal with a client and a part of me was made billable.

No wonder, the company that made $2 Billion USD in 2009, ended up making USD $16 Billion in 2019.

> Those who wonder why some companies grow and some struggle, must by now know the answer. You can grow only when you are not driven by your constraints. Understand them, consider them but act with an eye to the future. It is as simple as that.

This specific challenge of further growth is felt by literally every single company and the solution is always the same – invest in growth or forego it completely.

You could say, it is easy for a company to do – since what they lose is only shareholder's money. Majority of the wealth in the world today was created by companies and losing money or value is not something companies can afford in the long term or they will close down.

> We heard a true story shared by an investor in one of the wealth seminars. He was the chairman a school board and also an investor. As part of their investment strategy, the board decided to have 50% investment in stocks and 50% in bonds.
>
> He reckoned that this was a wise financial strategy and had been built with significant input from the experts, so he followed it in his personal life as well.
>
> As the bond market grew, he recommended that they sell the stocks and buy more bonds but school voted against that. Instead, to ensure they had alignment with 50-50 principle, they actually sold their bonds to bring the ratio of investment to 50-50.
>
> In the personal side, he reduced his investment in the shares and increased the ratio in favour of bonds – on paper, his money literally doubled!

However, next year, the share market started going up and the trend indicated further growth and similar argument was presented to board to sell the bonds and invest heavily in stocks. The board again decided to keep it aligned to the 50-50 strategy and sold the stocks to keep the ratio to 50-50.

On the personal side, he ended up reversing his position and sold bonds to buy stocks and became heavily leveraged on the stock side.

As the stock market crashed in 2008, he personally lost a fortune but the school funds were hedged well and were not affected.

There were 3 key learnings here

A. There is always a benefit of other people's insights.

B. Alignment with a thought-through strategy is beneficial in the long term.

C. Don't play with your money in the stock market based on your emotions.

Most of us do not ever worry about the cost of stupid decisions, emotional steps and not investing in ourselves.

However, the fact remains, that if we do not invest, we just cannot grow. And watching those amazing YouTube videos is the snail's pace of growth!

When it comes to investment in their career, most people cannot think beyond attending a university or increasing the technical skills or getting technical certifications.

All these things are important. We are not against that but if that's all you focus on, then you are doing a big mistake. You are focusing on something which is appreciated by the external world and not focusing on something which is going to lift you up internally.

What do we mean by external skills? Well, these are the skills, which are useful for you to execute the technical aspect of a job (PMP, Programming Language, Agile certification, etc.) and is valued by employers.

While all that is important, what is more important is how well you know yourself and how good you are in exhibiting it outside, as authentically as you can.

You may spend $3000 in learning that particular programming language but that experience is not going to give you $30,000 job right away. It is going to take a lot of time for you to get to that level. Probably you may even have to wait for a few years before you get promoted to that level where this skill will be useful.

Similarly doing some Microsoft certification or some security certification, all of those are not going to create results right away. In fact, you will have to apply to many jobs to get your foot in the door and after a point, it will be useless.

However, if you invest $10,000 on a personal development course, it is going to enhance your thinking by 10X and with that thinking, you will be able to easily secure better jobs and drive bigger results in much shorter time.

None of us were born with the total awareness of what is right and wrong. We learnt lessons along the way based on our experiences.

Unfortunately, for most adults, this process almost stops when they enter the corporate world and their interactions with their environment becomes limited to their jobs.

Stop to ask yourself this question – where is this learning you have had after you entered the job world, coming from?

"Interaction with my environment and people" – would be the most accurate response.

How do you know if it is not at snails' pace? The only way to find out what others are doing to grow themselves.

Invest in the books you read, the seminars you attend, the personal development journey you take. This will create an altogether different level of success than you would have seen in the past.

Invest in the future to create the success you desire.

Or stay stuck in the present!

Let us revise the plan that we laid out in the book and see how we are progressing

====

Chapter 1 is geared towards developing an understanding of how do we operate currently and what motivates our behaviour.

A deep understanding of this is critical because unless we observe the big picture of how we operate in life and how we react to the external environment, any solution otherwise will be tactical and doomed to fail unless you dwell upon segregating the pretences, we have been doing unknowingly due to a distorted understanding of what takes to be successful in the corporate environment.

====

What we have covered in this chapter is the challenge each of us face – with some strategies that can be used as a response.

It will be a lot of fun when we start learning HOW those strategies need to be implemented by leveraging our 7-step framework for personal growth.

Let us now get to the part of WHY we do these things.

====

Chapter 2 talks about WHY of what we do. It is important to understand the story of our deep-rooted beliefs and the reason for the specific ways we operate. Here we also look into the self-imposed obstacles and how do they impact our decisions in life.

====

Chapter 2

Getting Back to The Roots

"Many men go fishing all of their lives without knowing that it is not fish they are after"

– Henry David Thoreau

So far, we have seen that on one hand, we have these limiting beliefs and on the other hands, we have these specific circumstances that hold us back.

Kapil: 20 years into the Corporate world, I saw a significant change in me and my friends – well not overnight but over a period of time. The conversation slowly turned to how hard we were working and how much "less" we were earning and how others were becoming richer without working as hard as us.

And these "others" were always people who were either not as "smart" as we were or those who got "lucky" just like Mark Zuckerberg.

The delusion wasn't limited to my friends – I heard it being whispered almost everywhere- so much so that I started believing it myself. "If everyone is saying the same thing, it ought to be true."

What broke the camel's back was an episode of our first "foray" in business. Along with a friend, I discussed the possibility of business with Shyam, CEO of an IT service company in India, who wanted to start tapping into the Australian market.

That night, after that discussion with Shyam, my friend and I excitedly discussed the company name and other stuff for hours and that really made me feel very powerful.

Needless to say, nothing happened. Things didn't move an inch as we didn't take any action.

Shyam was very gracious. It seemed that in his 10 years as an entrepreneur, he must have seen this happen multiple times. He knew that there is a good chance that this conversation was born out of a passionate, motivational talk, that is unlikely to lead to action.

As I talked to more people, to my utter surprise, I found that the middle age crisis for our generation often takes that form of "I want to open my own business".

Since then, I have spoken to probably a hundred people and the crisis point always is similar.

Incidentally, what comes after that crisis is really depressing. Post that comes a cloak of contentment and being at peace with it!

"I am happy with what I have got!"

"I do not want to run after anything in life. I want to enjoy what I have"!

"I know I can do so much more but I don't need to, I am contented!"

The hell you are – you have given up!

You are contaminating the minds of your children who look at your busy, unproductive weekends. They look at your jobs where you either come home early or work sporadically long hours.

They hear your conversation with your friends about how jobs suck and how jobs are just a vehicle to earn your bread and butter.

You have arrived at an average game in life and you have become a master of deceit.

Only you know the heaviness- - as you try to make peace with it at 4 am in the morning. Only you know all the chains that are binding you to live up to your full potential.

How on earth can you run with all that weight that drags you down? How can you actually act as the CEO of your life with all those thoughts stopping you from flying high?

Let us just take this head on – why leave it to imagination?

Let us see how it impacts you.

Your life is/was/will be affected by your background and experiences. How you handle this, how you interpret it and most importantly, how you get past it will finally determine how well you grow in your career.

You may ask, what has this got to do with your career.

Where you are in your career is 99% a result of your background and experiences so far.

That governs how you react to your circumstances and things that are outside your control. It is those reactions that determine how well you do in your career.

Understanding your background, your stories, what has been limiting you and how you are leading your career between peaks of performance are the essential starting points to build an awesome career.

Living between these peaks seems to be something most people have accepted as a core strategy.

We all know people who have this average game at the core of their strategy. Very successful, they seem to jump around avoiding things that are even a little out of their knowledge circle and they stay well within their comfort zone!

These people often fit all definition of success. They have money, great house, good bank balance, their children go to a great school/university. Their days are filled with operational, transactional stuff that is hardly inspiring for anyone, let alone themselves.

For majority of them, work is just a way to get good money. And money is needed to stay in a beautiful house, live a comfortable life, watch a nice movie, spend time in trivialities and start the next day, the same way. Day after day, month after month, year after year!

"What is wrong with that?"

Since you are reading this book and have reached so far, we hope you don't even ask that question. If that is the extent of someone's ambition, would you really want to associated with such a person?

This average game can be beaten and life can be so much more, if the fire that made you pick up this book becomes a raging blaze to help you want to be the best version of yourself!

Let us jump right into your life, your past and your reality.

Then we will look at how we can change it.

YOUR CONTROL ON YOUR LIFE

> *"A person often meets his destiny on the road*
> *he took to avoid it."*

– Jean de La Fontaine

Your family, religion and even your name was decided before you were born. You came into this world in a passive mode, eating what you were fed and learning what you were taught.

A good part of your early years was spent in school, where you did not have the opportunity to feast on the subject that you loved because it was all about passing in all compulsory subjects for a well- rounded development, irrespective of your own interest. School boxed you nicely in a bright package that was best suited for the average challenges of life.

You did well in school or probably not so well and next came the university. It was a big deal as it was called by others as your gateway to the outside world. All the people who had any connection with you whatsoever, came into their best form to coax you to pick up a stream that will make you a corporate success.

You were the centre of every discussion on the dining table and on phones with the extended family. There was pride in those eyes on what you were accomplishing and how well behaved you were. In other words, as most people do and as most people accomplish.

Once again, the important decisions of your life were being taken without you having a say at it, and you allowed yourself to be thrown into an ocean of conventional wisdom, by joining that

Engineering, Medical or Accounting profession. After all, people around you wanted you to be successful and this "what everyone does" continued to be the ruling guideline.

But you were smarter than most and you figured there is something wrong – you decided to get to the top of the ladder by climbing higher and did post-graduation, which narrowed down the "everyone does it list" to a bare 10% than before.

You were then scooped up by a corporate giant, who came all the way to the campus to gobble you up before you got a chance to think about anything else. You again couldn't say no as you wanted to prove to others and yourself that you were so much in demand. Perhaps your personal circumstances, financial constraints, sense of responsibility played a role as you took the wise path because that is what someone who is responsible will do.

Once you entered corporate life, you were imprisoned for ever by the corporate zombies, promotions, free insurances and off course, that fat pay check in your bank account every month.

This was amazing as you contemplated what to do with the significant money you made and how much better it was than rest of your friends! You used some of that money to upgrade your technical skills as those were selling like hotcakes in the market and fewer people were doing it.

This paid back well. You went up the ladder and further shrank that comparative figure of the number of people in that top slot.

The rise to the top created a standard you had to live by- in the form of having a great partner, a palatial house and the best car in the market.

However, in your late thirties as you jumped from one shiny object to another, you started noticing that the shine disappears the moment you grab it.

None of it brought fulfillment.

You remembered your parents' wisdom how once you reach that level, which was impossible for them, it will bring in massive rewards and you knew that you had ticked all the boxes, yet you didn't feel like you won. Perhaps you needed to go beyond.

A little more time passed and then one evening, you recalled your school teacher's warning not to lose track of your dreams and you started feeling that she was on the verge of being proved right!

The weekends you live for.

The vacations that you wait for.

The hobby that you keep pushing off.

The dream that you have but seems far away.

All in exchange for

An average corporate zombie life that sucked all your happiness!

It is surely not possible to change now.

You can't just throw a well settled life for chasing your dreams. It will be childish. What would your family think, what would your son aspire, if he sees you acting so recklessly?

A wise friend whispers in your ear – "be contented".

Who are you to challenge that?

What are you but an average bloke who is doing amazing by the average standards of the society?

======================

As you read the above, it is likely to leave you angry, dejected, worried, anxious and with host of other emotions. The one that may keep returning is **Anger**.

Anger as to how you allow your life to be governed by others!

Anger as to how you follow the herd and bask in the glory of success for those short times – knowing fully in the back of your mind that this is not going to last!

Anger as to how the distorted meaning of the career growth has created an epidemic of sort, where people mindlessly run from one designation to others, never quite arriving anywhere!

Ask yourself, if your life is in your control.

If Life is not in your control, what makes you think, your career is?

So, if in a world, where decisions about your life has been taken by others, what can you do to take the control in your hand?

Accepting that your life and career choices were governed by others is the starting point for any change. Only then you would make effort to understand how you can change it.

Before we get into it, let us see how our experiences make an impact to our career and life in general.

THE STORY OF YOUR LIFE

"Do Not Judge, You Don't Know What Storm I've Asked Her to Walk Through"

– The Bible

At birth, the brain size is about a quarter of an adult brain. It doubles in the first year and keeps growing, reaching 90% of its size by year 5. Brain is the only organ in human body, which does not produce new cells once it is developed (by year 25).

However, it is not the number of neurons that matters, it is the connection between them, that gives us our intellect, our abilities and our extraordinary powers.

The connection between neurons are made from our day to day interactions and the process continues till we die. However, when we are young, about 1 million connections (called synapses) are made every second. It may seem too large a number, but imagine, the number of synapses in a 3 year' old baby is about 1 quadrillion (1000 trillion) and an adult has about 500 trillion synapses.

A baby learns from every single thing and acts like a savant – in terms of noticing everything. The way our brain develops these connections is a simple process. When impulses (as a response to external stimuli), pass from one neuron to others, there is a connection created resulting in a new memory. What makes them a long-term connection is the repeatability of the experience as repeated use strengthens the Synapsys.

At 3 years of age, a baby has about 200% more Synapses than an adult brain. At that age however, something odd happens. The connections start breaking and continues to break till mid-20s.

Why would the brain do such a terrible thing? Create those connections and then break it!

It may feel like a terrible thing as it directly impacts associations that have been created in past – but this is a critical part of development as an adult. This is the fine-tuning process needed to ensure survival and environmental adoption.

During this time, unused Synapsys are broken. The way to understand it is, a child will notice every letter in each word till that age – but in order to understand a word, none of us have to know positioning of each letter in the word. This is evident from the fact that really young children will have massive difficulty in reading this sentence but an adult will find it very easy.

"It deosn't mttaer in waht oredr the ltteers in a wrod are, the olny iprmoetnt tihng is taht the frist and lsat ltteer be at the rghit pclae."

Still, losing the synapses may feel like a loss to some – so let us consider it. The Savant, who remember everything are not considered fully grown individuals as they are the people whose connections didn't break as much past that 3 year of age. They have difficulty in even tying their shoe laces because tying your shoelaces is a very complex process.

Synaptic pruning as it is called, is a critical development process and is known to be linked with autism.

You now understand the process of learning and have at least a high-level overview of the biological process. It is now easier to understand that our experiences that shape us also result in problematic synaptic connections, that impact how we deal with the world.

Problematic connections in my head? Some would gasp!

Yes, the experiences you have had, are "physically present" in your brain in the form of those Synapses. It is easy to see that once a correlation is made in our brain about a specific experience, any repeat instance will firm up the correlation, resulting in a learning that "this is the way life is".

Given the brain's propensity in early age to build the connections and the fact that the Synaptic pruning continues till about 25, it is possible to completely misunderstand events around us and create meaning where there is none.

Kapil: When I was 8 years old, my father used to work for a famous textile company and we lived in a 2-bedroom apartment on first floor of a large colony, which was like a paradise where thousands of other people lived in an enclosed, safe facility.

After years of living there, dad got a slightly bigger apartment when he got promoted.

This one had a large open area in front of it with a bit of greenery, trees and a "better" view.

The day we got the key, we decided to go there to spend the night. There was an electricity outage and the hot April day wasn't really helpful.

I decided to leverage my considerable level of creativity and went home to pick up a cricket stump, few ropes and a heavy bedsheet.

While rest of the family was in the other room with the fan (which wasn't working because of no electricity), I came to the larger room, which had only a hook in the ceiling for the fan.

Using a ladder, I put the rope through the hook and tied the two ends at the side of the stump.

Next, I put the blanket on the stump to make a hanging fan, that I could move using other pieces of loosely hanging rope. I moved it few times and felt the rush of air.

Extremely proud of myself, I ran to the other room and announced that they must all come to the large room. Everyone followed me and I showed my proud invention.

I don't remember what others said but I never forgot what my dad said.

He looked at me incredulously and said, "Are you crazy"?

My world fell apart!

That statement hit me harder than anything I could have imagined. Somehow that created a picture in my mind that I had to get his approval at all cost.

It became my life's biggest need and my way of life.

It may sound odd but the 8 year' old didn't know any better. That little boy created meaning in that statement, which was just a sudden reaction.

Having a twin brother, which is otherwise one of the most beautiful gifts of life, didn't really help the cause. He used to fall sick quite often– thus demanding more care and attention. I needed to make an effort to garner attention and ensuring that I get dad's approval, became my world.

Yet, the approval never came. I just had to reach a little more but it was forever a moving target.

And without me knowing about it, the known devil of never-quite-getting-the-approval became a way of life and continued at home, at the school, at the university, at the b-school, at work and in life for next 37 years.

My world became limited to working to get the approval but stopping before the approval actually came.

Why?

Because I didn't know the world that existed beyond that approval need.

I became absolutely great at initiating stuff but not finishing it.

Much later, one of my managers, Madhu, who later became a very dear friend, said it in an interesting way, "you are like this guru, who would spell-bound everyone with what you say for 55 minutes but will do something extremely odd in the last 5 min, to then make them reject everything you said earlier!"

The very thing I wanted most, I **acted** to not achieve it. If I did, the "want" would get fulfilled and "the drive" would disappear.

And what will I live for then? – I was so habitual of NOT being recognised for my "Guru" behaviour. Being recognised would have meant stepping into completely unknown!

A lot of people do that to their life. They shun away love, despite wanting it badly because they are forever in the domain of **reaching out but not quite getting there.**

I did finally get the approval of my dad but only when I completely stopped looking for it.

When I quit my corporate career, I fully expected my dad to say – "Big Mistake" – but all he said was, "I have full confidence in you. I know you will figure it out!"

VERY unusual for an Indian parent to say that in light of the drastic step I had taken.

Don't get me wrong – I love my dad and he is my best mate – he also provided me his unconditional love and an amazing environment all my life.

But that 8 year' old boy didn't know any better. That boy had to create a STORY of simple act of misplaced statement from daddy dear!

Each of us have a story.

When we were small, either our parents or siblings said something unknowingly or our friends laughed at something or there were unnecessary comparisons or there was a really bad incident that happened in our life, like a sexual abuse or growing up in a violent household.

And while all of those things are bad – some significantly more than others, it is how we carry them that impacts us **today**.

There are many people in the world who got over their stories. These people accepted them, they discussed with others and then went on to create and live their beautiful lives.

However, unfortunately, there are a significantly greater number of people who **never** make an effort to understand their stories and therefore could never get them out of their head!

What kind of person do you want to be?

You may ask, what has it got to do with growing in your career or getting promoted faster?

It has **everything** to do with that.

Promotion or career growth is NOT in isolation to WHO YOU ARE. If it is something you want to see happening once in a life time and not again, you may want to put this book down and hire a charlatan to create a massive story about you and get some visibility and connect with some people and somehow get you there.

But once you are there, you will fail.

Because unless you get rid of your story, you will carry the same person you are today, to that future job and role.

And how differently do you expect that person to perform in that space?

Shilpa: One of my mentees, who was extremely successful in corporate world, created his entire life around work. When he engaged with me, the entire thought was about how to grow in his career further.

Something didn't quite add up in our first session and soon our discussion went to other aspects of life, where only thing I could see was chaos and disturbance. He continued to maintain that he is able to keep his personal and professional life separate – till I finally managed to get his permission to talk to his partner.

What I discovered was a realisation for both him and for me.

All his personal relationships, all his discussions with friends and even with his partner were about work. His entire life was just focused on work.

The lack of balance, lack of harmony finally had started impacting his work – the thing he loved most – or so he thought.

As we dug deeper, almost all our discussions for 3 weeks became about the stories he had told himself. One specifically stood out and later turned out to be the core reason of why he chose this life. In short, when he was about 9 year' old, he was badly beaten up by some children at school, who happen to be from very rich families.

And he made his entire life about getting back at them by himself being very successful.

2 months later, his life transformed completely – he didn't give up on his dreams in the corporate life, but actually started moving with much more focus and energy, and with the right reasons.

His partner told me recently that their day to day interactions within themselves, with friends and family are now filled with so much joy and happiness about the present moments!

Is this a gift you also want to give yourself?

"Reach out to us at info@scintillate.com.au to see how we can work with you to help you live powerfully."

This book is for those who want to take complete control of their career, who want to get to the next level and move faster, with a much sharper focus and clarity.

It is the winning mindset that will get you there and also make it sustainable to get victorious in all other areas of life.

We will cover it in later sections of the book.

YOUR EXPERIENCES

"I have never met a strong person with an easy past"

– Unknown

A Human being has about 48 thoughts a minute. That is about 50,000 thoughts a day during the waking hours. 90% of these thoughts are about the same thing (There is a repeated pattern in our life that we constantly think about and follow).

Further, 10% of this (500 per day) are unique. Imagine yourself engaging with people with each of them buzzing with unique ideas and thoughts, with you too having your own unique ideas and thoughts. It's mind numbing to even consider the complexity of the interactions and the possibilities of conflicts that are bound to arise.

Consider a life time, if you are in your 30s, it would mean at least 20 years of conscious choices, thoughts, ideas. That is about 3.65 Million unique thoughts!

That is a lot of traffic. All of these experiences will absolutely shatter anyone unless there is a mechanism to handle this. And we all do have a mechanism. But for most of us, these mechanisms are never thought through.

Kapil: In January 2017, I walked into a local medical shop in Sydney to purchase medicines for my mum-in-law, who was visiting us from India.

The guy at the counter was an Asian Australian. He smiled as he looked at the list, mumbling something along the lines of "diabetes again!"

My rather stern look made him explain that for years, he'd been fascinated by the fact that diabetes was pretty much a "man-made disease" and how a large number of people from the Indian subcontinent ended up having it because of their eating habits.

We ended up having a fascinating discussion for the next 2 hours as he doled out wisdom about eating habits.

I didn't know it then – that was the inflection point for me. As I allowed myself to be swept by someone else's passionate knowledge and wisdom, I started challenging myself in ways I hadn't done before.

What followed was a series of small changes, each building on top of each other, very different from the haphazard manner in which I had lived until then.

These small droplets of water became a raging torrent over the last three years, touching every part of my life in ways that has left me surprised and beyond grateful.

A lot of us live our life in an automatic mode – playing ball by ball, letting events drive our lives, allowing day to day priorities to take control over our actions.

This entire automatic mode works for a majority of things we do daily but really hurts us in the long term, as many of these actions we take, have to be more thought through and deliberate.

The need for each of us therefore, is to turn it on its head and become deliberate about learning from other people's experiences instead of letting our own ones drive everything we do.

Shilpa: Few days back, I was on my walk in a park near my house and noticed that some hurdles have been setup, for a race that was about to begin.

As I saw the participants warming up, noticed that were from all age groups- from 12-year-olds to adults in their mid-forties. Intrigued, I stopped by to observe it closely.

As the race began, I noticed that younger the participant, the more effective they were in crossing the hurdles as they would try different tricks and techniques or just throw themselves in the air, without any fear of falling.

This enabled them to go much faster than the older participants, who ran with their bodies closed, carefully assessing risk before each hurdle, and obviously going slower, while covering a much shorter distance.

Isn't that exactly how we act in life, as we grow older?

When we were young, we did not know failure. We did not have experiences that would scare us from reaching out to people. We did not know that unless we do certain things in a certain way, we wouldn't succeed. We were not yet exposed to people, who would constantly remind us of how life sucks.

The dreams that we had once when we were young did not just die – they crumbled away beneath these heavy weights of worldly obstacles, as and when we got to know them..

It is rightly said that we learn the most from our failures and experiences – and such is the bane of this otherwise positive statement, that failure imprints in our mind as something to keep clear of rather than the real opportunity it presents.

Those hard-learnt lessons – when 1 out of 100 betrayed us and that one person became a representation of how most people are. The 'avoidance of pain' set in as a core principle.

If only it can be replaced with a more prudent "make a conscious choice and then own the responsibility" – more internal focused than external.

Those hard-learnt lessons – when lots of hard work just didn't lead anywhere. The "don't try too hard" sets in as a core principle.

If only it was replaced with the more prudent "don't keep doing the same thing, but do learn from it and adjust as needed" – more outcome driven than behaviour driven.

Those hard-learnt lessons – when our choices hurt someone else unintentionally and we felt worthless ourselves. Our mind learnt "let people have their space, don't bother them much."

If only it was replaced with "repair your past by acknowledging and asking for forgiveness and then setting it aside – and continue to engage with people. You won't get it right all the time" – more forward looking than self-beating.

Those hard-learnt lessons – when we had accidents or unfortunate events outside our control, it created another complex layer of learning that "life is not in my control."

If only it was replaced with "there will be lots of external factors that I won't be able to control, but I need to press on to get the best for myself" – more action oriented than constraint driven.

Those hard-learnt lessons – our situations, which sometimes meant limited opportunities for education or limited expressions of language or learning, added another dimension of "I am not enough" or "I am too young/too old/under educated/too educated"

If only it was replaced with "I will always figure out what to do" – more results focused than problem oriented.

Hand on heart, tell yourself the truth this time. Haven't you been there?

We may think that these negative learnings keep us safe. That is that little voice constantly whispering in your ear about why you shouldn't try new changes that have the potential to change your life for good.

In fact, a small habit will make a big difference. If you start writing decisions you take for a week, every single one of them, you will discover that there are too many times that you tell yourself why something **shouldn't be done;** and that is because of avoidance of attached pain rather opportunity of something bigger.

Those experiences that you had, have not served you well and they continue to constrain your life.

You have put a self-imposed exile from your pathway to excellence by giving too much importance to those experiences.

Till you continue to hang on to that; your growth will be constrained.

YOUR LIMITING BELIEFS- CHAINING YOU, HOLDING YOU BACK

"If you accept a limiting belief,
then it will become a truth for you."

– Louise L. Hay

Kapil: When I was young, I lived in an industrial city called Kota in Rajasthan, India. My dad worked in a big textile company. We lived in this beautiful, safe, enclosed colony, where each evening, you could meet hundreds of people going for a walk and really positive and animated discussions every night as if there was a party going on!

When I was 11-year-old, my dad's company retrenched thousands of people. While my dad's job was saved, the safe colony that I lived in became an intoxicating place due to massive negative sentiments around how the owners were out to suck blood from the common people.

While I have not bothered around getting to the root of how and why, I distinctly remember the depressing conversations, adults huddled around dimly lit street lamps. The negative vibes kept spreading as families after families started departing from the safe haven of the Colony, which only a few years back was one of the most vibrant places in the world for me.

As a child, I walked away with one feeling.

Rich people are bad. And an automatic interpretation was having richness is bad. "People who make money do it at the cost of poor people".

The constant onslaught of the drama in the Hindi movies of 80s and 90s continued to reinforce this baseless belief that didn't hurt me directly.

But evidences kept piling up!

Much later, this got into a full-blown belief that money is the root of all evils.

Laughingly, this was despite the fact that I intellectually dived into Ayn Rand in 90s, whose teachings were completely opposite.

I assimilated these two, opposing points of view as – "as long as I am making money for others, it is good".

Without going into any more details, this impacted my relationship with money and I kept getting back to the base that money is the root of all evils.

This impacted me massively.

I am not the only one with this distorted sense of the world of richness, money, affluence. Each one of us have certain belief about how the world is.

For some, the world is full of people who are out to get them or people who do not want others to be successful.

For some, the world is run by some hidden sources and as long as you keep them happy, it will all work.

For some, the corporates are out to suck the blood out of them and let them hang.

For some, the world is a cruel place, where you have to get armed mentally and the get into the arena, where every battle has to be won.

We can go on and on about how many irrational beliefs, our mind is filled with and how most do not make any sense.

Because in each of them, YOU stand apart as the source of all good and all things right.

For some, even that core of who they are is corrupted and they know, they have to play it tough all the time – almost like, being evil as a choice – as our movies show us!

There are umpteen number of these limited beliefs that you and I acquired when we were growing up.

The story of your life created a certain personality, which interpreted that experience with the eyes of a small child and decided how the world is. That child's interpretation runs the world for you even today.

This one single realisation can set your life in a different direction.

You may be thinking that given all the great accomplishments you have had – there isn't a chance in the world that such limiting beliefs exist in your mind. Let us discuss how they get created.

As we shared in Chapter 1, there are two driving force for all human behaviour.

Why we do what we do is because we either want to:

1. avoid the pain of something that arises out of not doing it or

2. get the pleasure of doing something and getting a reward

If you notice, every advertisement that you see, uses either of the above (pain or pleasure) to drive people to action.

What drives you more?

We have asked this question personally to at least 100 people and most people start with 2 but once challenged, settle for 1.

It seems simple but we are 10 times more likely to do things to avoid pain than have pleasure.

Why?

Human brain evolved to keep us safe. Majority of life of homo sapiens and others animals has been in the wild where the danger to life is incredible. Our amygdala specifically evolved to keep us safe.

That is why when you meet a stranger, your hind brain is quickly evaluating if you are safe. Your neocortex does take control eventually but the first reactions come from the hind brain.

As a matter of fact, there are 7 filters that we quickly go through when we are in a situation that is unfamiliar – which incidentally is 100% time when we try something different or break new barriers.

The 7 filters are:

- Does it look dangerous?
- Is there a possibility of failure?
- Can I do it?
- Is it even worth trying?
- Am I getting into uncertainty?
- Is there any complication I may get into?
- Will this be boring?

Only when the above instincts are managed, handled and removed, can someone move to the next stage of interaction with the environment. For that, you have to fight this first response to act to avoid the pain.

While it may look simple, this often is responsible for creating havoc in life.

Imagine being in early career and being ripped to shreds by a bad manager for every single piece of bad communication you had. You could end up with a limiting belief that "I need to perfect everything and then only I must share with others."

We have met with a lot of people who actually narrowed down their career challenges to this single sentence.

The whole idea then becomes how to avoid the pain of being ripped off by others.

Many people never take the first step towards a brilliant insight because of this thought, "once I start it, I must do it perfectly, otherwise I will be ripped to pieces" and there is never enough time to make it perfect.

Too many such brilliant, world changing ideas are buried under the rubble of fear and inaction.

Many times, the avoidance of pain also creates a massive impetus to do things— because not doing something will create so much pain that it will be a bigger problem!

The other critical parameter here is the need of the hour. Our brain is unfortunately not evolved to consider long term pain. If only it was, we will become so wise and always choose the right option with our long-term perspective in mind.

The fact is that it takes a lot of mental muscles to consider our long-term prospects. These mental muscles can be built up only if we don't let our natural tendency of focus on avoiding immediate pain or getting immediate pleasure and become deliberate in making choices.

Shilpa: About 14 years back, we were staying in an apartment in Hyderabad, where I had built an excellent support system around our full-time jobs and our 5-year-old and 2-year-old daughters. We were surrounded by our reliable family- a nanny, a cook, a cleaner and a security watchman, all of them, ready to help us with anything and everything, whenever needed.

That apartment was extremely beautiful and its walls were painted with different colours of love (bright red, orange, yellow and blue) by myself and Kapil, when we were 7 months pregnant with our second child.

However, with an easy access to all facilities (hospital, parlour, school, grocery and a family crèche), it was in a busy marketplace and not having a park nearby for the kids was a challenge, something that we could definitely compromise on but it certainly would have added a huge value to their growing years.

I heard about a fantastic gated community coming up within 6 kms of our house, with excellent facilities like a swimming pool, 6 fully equipped playgrounds, a shopping mall and a community centre. The new area wasn't as well connected to the transport as we would have liked and the support system that existed for us wasn't really a possibility.

Our choice was to decide to move to that new facility or stick to where we were comfortably staying, well protected with our fantastic support system.

Now you may be thinking that it was pretty evident that the new place promised opportunities like none other and it should have been an easy choice.

But what pulled me back was the pain of leaving a well settled support system, where I could trust anyone with anything, at any point of time.

I still remember Kapil and I having a discussion about it one day – we actually created an excel sheet with pros and cons with weighted average – a little overboard – but you see, we were still building our mental muscles for making deliberate choices.

The detailed evaluation gave way to a quick decision.

We decided to move in pursuit of better opportunities for our daughters and guess what, it turned out to be the best decision of our lives.

We got an opportunity to stay in the best area of the city, with the state-of-the-art facilities inside the campus and multitudes of extra-curricular activities for kids right under our nose, excellent school bus connectivity and Kapil's new office 10 min away!

And the biggest challenge of not having a support system was easily solved by hiring a full-time housekeeper to help us with everything, including kids. We bought another car to resolve the connectivity issue!

And soon we were reaping rewards of our decisions.

Simple!

Looking back at your life, you too can find many such events and decisions where you took a path and it turned out to be fine.

In fact, every single thing you do will turn out fine.

The path not taken is the path not taken. Don't worry about it, don't fret on it, don't let it define your future – in any shape or form.

In most cases, we hold on to the present as our most precious possession, which makes the pain of parting with it look much bigger than the opportunity ahead. But once we see the long-term benefits and commit to adopt the change, we can effectively welcome the opportunity with open arms.

Everything falls in place, in most cases, much better than the present.

PEAK PERFORMANCE – AND HOW IT DOES <u>NOT</u> DEFINE YOU

"If you are always trying to be normal,
you will never know how amazing you can be."

– Maya Angelou

Kapil: "We will not be offering you the job of the Program Manager that you applied for", Vani said.

My heart sank - this was something unexpected as I had actually cracked the interview and Microsoft was THE dream company I wanted to work for.

For 5 years, I had worked for smaller companies in India and it wasn't very uplifting for me to tell people that I work for a company *called* ABC, some unheard name.

Back then, I compared myself with others - especially other engineering and MBA batchmates, who worked for large, well-known global brands. There was a significant confusion and massive disposition towards working for a big name!

Applying for Microsoft was born out of partly desperation and partly because I had just heard about "Affirmations" from Scott Adams's book (of Dilbert Fame).

"What-is-there-to-lose" is how I thought.

When I got the call for a telephonic interview with US, I managed to convince a telephone booth operator to give me his office for 2 hours to make an international call.

It was a smooth one and I knew I would sail through other rounds.

After clearing few more rounds of interviews on the phone, I was asked to fly over to Hyderabad for a final round of video conference with the hiring managers in Redmond, USA and soon the paper ticket for the flight was delivered to my home.

As it happens, my flight got 4 hours late and I landed at Hyderabad airport at 11:30 PM in the night. The taxi was waiting for me and we rushed through the still wide-awake Hyderabad roads to the Microsoft office in Hi-Tech City to the majestic Cyber Tower. It was a painful travel seated at the back of an ambassador, that could do a max 45 KMPH!

Vani, the HR person, was waiting for me and ushered me into a conference room, handed me a cold drink, a water bottle and within minutes, the interview started with 8-9 people on the other side of the world.

"I am sorry for the delay", I started - but one of the persons in the interview quipped, "if you could control the airline times in India, we will immediately hire you".

That put me at ease and the next 1.5 hours were a smooth sail.

I really thought I nailed it when they informed me that they have to do a Technical round that should take an hour but were being kicked out of the conference room. They asked me to get the HR Manager (Vani) quickly so that they could arrange for the next round.

I bolted out of the conference room, couldn't find Vani anywhere so went **out** to the reception to ask for her.

There was a security guard at the reception, half asleep. It was night 2 AM and Vani obviously had gone home!

All I had to do was to call Vani. But the door back inside the office, I just came out of was locked.

"Can you open it?"

"Sir, I don't have the key"

"Can you call Vani"

"Sir, we don't have her number"

"Can you give me access to a computer?"

The guy looked at me as if I was mad!

So here I was, locked outside - my phone, my wallet inside, stuck at 2 AM outside an office.

I had to do something and did the only thing I could – I started calling all the 4 digits intercom numbers. Fortunately, the first two numbers were fixed – so it was a matter of dialling it only 99 times!

Easy!

Finally, what seemed like an eternity, someone picked up the phone - one of those committed Microsoft Developers who was in office at that ungodly hour. And just like that, I was through the first hoop of getting inside the office to grab my phone.

I tried calling Vani from my phone – her phone was switched off.

My saviour gave me a laptop and I found Vani's mail in my inbox, which contained the name of the hiring manager. I was back in the game!

I looked up the guy on outlook and called him. No response.

For next 45 min, I must have made 40-50 calls and must have spoken to 10-15 people but to no avail.

"Do those folks ever sit in their office or all the time in meetings?" I wish I had known back then how true that was!

Finally, after what seemed like another eternity, one person said, "yes, entire building no 27 is talking about a guy from India calling up everyone about his interview and the hiring manager. They will be sending you mail shortly".

I am sure he exaggerated! I couldn't have suddenly become so popular!

To this day, I don't know why that hiring manager didn't send me a mail in the first place! Maybe he gave up as the norm for most people is to postpone it till next time!

The technical interview had only 2 people - it was around 4 AM. The first questions, this hiring manager asked me, "how did you find us" and I narrated my story.

For some reasons, I still remember the next question and my response. He asked, "What made you keep trying and not letting it organised later?" and I said, "no reasons – I just had to keep going" – I thought it was a very smart answer!

I regretted it the moment I heard them say, "Hmmm, ok, we don't have any other question".

I also regretted the fact that my first ever 5-star experience was cut short to a quick bath, 1-hour breakfast and rush back to airport to catch an 8:30 AM flight.

As the aircraft landed and I switched on my huge Nokia, I got a call from Vani.

"We will not be offering you the job of the Program Manager that you applied for", Vani said.

My dreams were shattered and shoulders hunched down but she continued, "We will be offering you role of the Senior Program Manager role".

> There, I had made it.... something I so badly wanted that there
> was no other option.

====

Reflecting back, this was a power packed, peak performance. Each and every one of us had those days.

Here is what we want you to do:

Write down 5 instances in your career when you delivered peak performance, where you showed the mettle of who you are.

_____

_____

_____

_____

_____

The 5 peak times you wrote – there are massive hidden gems in there.

When you think of those instances of peak performance - some of the things that you will notice about yourself are:

A. **Resourcefulness** – when you accomplished that – you were resourceful

B. **Resilience** – you didn't stop despite setbacks, issues and blockers, that otherwise would be daunting

C. **Relationships** – you either leveraged relationships or you found that you ended up creating new, powerful ones

In other words, when you WANT to, when you REALLY want to – you are able to get over ANY obstacles.

This is a very simple but a powerful thought.

These peaks indicate that you are capable of achieving greatness **when you want to** – but the life you have lived, these peaks end up being just peaks – effervescent, not lasting!

We are absolutely sure that if you think more deeply, you can write 15-20 of those.

These peak moments were the true peak moments. And those peak moments are significantly responsible for what you accomplished so far in your career.

However, here is the cracker.

If you add up all the efforts that you made during those peak moments and all the glory that came with it – it will barely add to about 5% of your career.

95% of your life has been without peak performance. 95% has been average.

There are 3 possible responses to this.

Response number One, **Denial** – *"The figure has to be wrong."* Or *"That is the way world is."* Or *"You cannot have it all."*

That is not going to help you. The rule stands – THE GAME YOU HAVE BEEN PLAYING HAS BEEN AN AVERAGE GAME.

But here is the good news!

Once you get past this realisation, you can change the game. You can decide consciously to live your life in a way that you can experience significantly more number of these peak moments.

This doesn't mean running after a mirage of high performance. It means, finding meaning, purpose, strengths in day to day life and playing it full in all aspects of life.

Response number Two, **Acceptance**, which is *"yes, such is the nature of life"* that would create a level of despondency that we seek to resolve in this book.

This emerges from a blatant realisation that all the time we have spent worrying about our career– even with that, we have a life that is 95% spent below average.

How would your life be, if this 95% could come down to 40-50%?

Where would your finances be?

Where would your relationships be?

Where would your health be?

Response number Three, **Massive surprise,** *"really, 95% below average?"* welcome to the real world!

In all the three circumstances, it is most likely that to stay insane, you say that is how life is and it is not possible to change, etc., etc.

And that thinking is what keeps you caged and keeps your life average.

Is that how high performers think?

If you want to get promoted faster and if you want to get there in a sustainable way and not as a one-off tactical growth, **you have to play the game at a much bigger level.**

The first rule is to **play with all your heart** –invest all your energy and focus on raising your game in life and operate at a completely different level.

A pre-requisite is to let go of this belief that there is some unknowable order in the world that needs your life to be lived at 95% down and 5% peak.

That is the only way to move forward towards that big objective you want.

Let us revise the plan that we laid out in the book and see how we are progressing

====

Chapter 1 talks about how do we do things currently and what is the issue with that. This chapter is geared towards developing an understanding of our motivations and how we operate. A deep understanding of this is really critical as any solutions otherwise will be tactical and doom to fail unless you dwell upon segregating the pretences, we have been doing unknowingly due to a distorted understanding of what takes to be successful in the corporate environment.

Chapter 2 talks about WHY of what we do. It is important to understand the story of our deep-rooted beliefs and reasons of the specific way we operate. Here we also look into the self-imposed obstacles and how they impact our decisions in life.

====

We are done with these two and we hope that you have a deep awareness of your challenges and things that you want to change along with few strategies of how to handle it.

It is now time for getting into the underlying structure of these strategies and refine it to make a practical and implementable approach you can take.

Some of you may be wondering that this book is not just about career.

You are right.

We come from a fundamental premise that you cannot make big changes in life and live a life of passion unless you make changes in who you are. Following the strategies in this book will not just give you a 1000X return, if you could measure it, it will also bring alive an unknown power inside you that will make anything and everything possible!

PART 2

Chapter 3
Building Blocks

"Brick by Brick my fellow citizen, brick by brick"

– Emperor Hadrian

When a great fire destroyed the ancient Rome, people asked Emperor Hadrian, how they are going to build the city back, he responded with the above sentence, that will always be held true – no matter how much time passes.

The system is always the same. You keep putting one above the other. You keep doing it till the entire wall is built.

A lot of people have lost the meaning of it though. In today's well-connected world, where everything is out there in open for all to see, majority of us see the big successes but miss out on all the hard work that goes behind it.

There is an overnight success formula that people are desperately searching for. There has to be one, because Uber, Airbnb, even FB were simple ideas. Too many of us have tried since then to develop that one fantastic application that can attract the masses and that will convert us into an overnight success!

And while almost everyone failed at it, Netflix squeezed in, Vyom was created, Tesla was born. Even the Fortnite game guy made billions.

Most people keep looking for THE success formula.

There is definitely a success formula. And it is hidden in the deep core of each of us. It is who you were born to be. It is that discovery of yourself.

It starts with creating building blocks for the life you want to build.

These blocks will not be the one that will suck life out of you as you implement them, they will **infuse** life into you. These would create a meaning in your life where your success is assured.

Yes, **assured**, you read it right. Your **assured** success! These are big claims. But here is our big promise to you, as you read through, you will realise how easy it is.

The building blocks are described in this chapter.

These will create a life architecture so powerful that implementing them will mean that you will be able to play it full in every single domain in life!

In a nutshell, these will provide you a deep understanding of **Why?** **How?** And **What?**

HAPPINESS – FOCUS ON WHY?

"Any fool can know, the point is to understand"

– Albert Einstein

No matter who you are, what you do, what have you accomplished, each of us want joyful happiness at the core of our existence.

There is a lot of philosophical content about this in literature. Instead of giving a theoretical foundation, we want to cover our experiences, experiences of people we know and the people we have mentored.

No one wants to have tons of money and be unhappy. No one wants to be popular and be unhappy. No one wants to have great health and be unhappy.

Different people have different definitions of what happiness is for them. Some people say, it comes from giving and contributing. Some say, it comes from giving oneself to a higher power. For some, they see their parents being contented with what they got and call that happiness. Some people see children being in the moment and consider that as happiness.

They are all right.

A lot of you would know that story where a management consultant sees a person at a lake catching fishes.

"You are catching all these fishes! Man, you are good! Why don't you consider getting a bigger fishing rod, you can catch more fishes!"

"Why should I do that" The man says.

The management consultant continues, "then you can actually sell them and get a few more rods that you can hire other people to catch fishes for you, which you can then sell at a profit"

"Why should I do that" The man says.

The management consultant continues, "you can then get a boat and catch fishes in a river where there are more fishes- before you know, you would be able to buy a trailer and will be catching lots of fishes in the sea"

"Why should I do that" The man says.

The management consultant is now excited, "you will be rich and then can do whatever you want with your time.

"That is what I am doing now!" The man says.

This story has been probably one of the most cited examples by many contented people. It is almost that they are saying, "Why play it big when small makes you happy?"

Why indeed? A lesson on happiness cannot be completed till we get this out of the way.

You may ask, what is the problem if that person is actually happy catching fishes.

In **Ignorance**, you do not know the **possibilities** that exist for you and for your loved ones. When you are aware of those and living your life so that you can continuously move towards those possibilities, the level of happiness is completely different. It is sustainable, it is replenishable and it is based on the true joy of creating something worthwhile.

Would you rather be happy in ignorance or in awareness?

Happiness is not a destination – it is not "catching fishes". It is a journey- **a journey is about progression**. Staying in the same place and being happy continuously is highly incongruent.

Don't get us wrong, being in a moment and being happy is not a question here – that is indeed the entire idea.

It is the sustainability of that happiness, that constant realisation that you are progressing and moving forward, makes it sustainable.

There is a great story about Deepak Chopra, who decided to attend 2 weeks of monk's journey – around 2018. As a part of this, he had to go for alms round, asking villagers for food. As the story goes, he had significant hardship walking barefoot on rocky path, full of bristles and thorns.

He went to his guru, a young monk in his twenties and told him "Putting every foot on the sun-baked path is a torture and I am just not finding it good."

The monk asked "how about when you lift the foot"?

This was a moment of revelation for him as he found new joy with every step he took and focused on raising his foot off the ground.

You may ask, where is the continuity in that? Where is the achievement and progression?

Consider it again. He was able to concentrate on that small movement. putting one foot in front of each. When you do that, the senses become sharper; you notice everything.

It was his forward movement, his advancement of the senses, his progress.

Also, taking this in isolation may feel like "this is it". But not quite. Let us not fool ourselves that this was the only source of fulfilment and this is the way to live forever!

Being able to go to each moment in life and savour it, creates an ability to look at the big picture, in ways that was not possible before. This increased ability leads to progress and it is the progress that brings true joy.

Each of us have to move forward in life. How fast you move is up to you.

"Joy and Happiness Emerge from Progress"

– Tony Robbins

When you look at a toddler being happy playing with small toy – it is the progress of knowing something new that make him happy.

When you see a young girl falling in love with someone – it is that feeling of new discovery, of forward progress that makes her happy.

When you see a middle-aged man discover his true passion, it is that feeling of internal power of knowing and seeing the future possibilities that make him happy.

When you see an old woman spending time in tendering her garden, it is seeing that the plants are being nurtured and growing in her care that makes her happy.

At the core of any happy moment is PROGRESS. **Without progress, sustainable happiness is not possible.**

We challenge you to consider ANY moment in your life and see that the while happiness was in the moment, the feeling become long lasting only when you saw that source of happiness as progress.

Be it a new car, a new phone or a new laptop, each of those moments was about progress in life. Acquiring material good itself is not progress – it is that **ability** to buy that gives you long-lasting happiness.

When you help someone – it is not some superiority that makes you happy, it is that privilege that you feel **being in the position of a giver**.

Happiness is not a short-term kick that we get when we achieve something. It is built-up of a belief about ourselves that we are worth it when we are able to acquire something.

Happiness is not about achieving things per se or Robin Williams would have never committed suicide. A lot of successful people get bored and sad, when they perceive they are not growing.

While progress will always make us happy, the reverse is also true. Lack of progress will always make you feel terrible.

Is there one single path to our happiness?

No. However, there is a path and it is the path **you** decide. And if you are like most people, you know that for a very long time, your path was decided by your constraints and reactions to the external circumstances.

Now, when our attention is turned towards Progress, let us consider where does this progress come from?

"Progress Comes from Focused Actions"

As we grow in life, we look up to people, who are successful.

Everyone you admire, has that edge, that spark, that characteristic that you want to see within yourself.

Those successful people really have the knowledge. Everyone talks about them.

And it makes us believe, Knowledge is the key. We then spend decades gathering knowledge. Our social beliefs fuel that fire further and we end up getting a lot of knowledge but we still don't become like those super successful people we admire.

Those successful people were spoken about because they were visible and known. And they weren't visible and known for their knowledge alone – they were visible because they actually **did** something. They took actions. Not just actions but **focused** actions to create powerful results.

In order to progress in life, you must take focused actions. When you think of "Focus", there is a direction that immediately pops up in the picture. This is something we will further discuss in this chapter.

Yet, most people don't take enough concerted actions towards their intended results.

"Everyone worries about the intermittent problems– If only they do it with focus and long enough – they will be propelled to action"

- Kapil K

Our limiting beliefs come in the way of taking those focused actions.

A few times, when we do something different, it was in response to the external environment and barely ever as a **conscious choice!**

Shilpa: As part of her growing years, our daughter, Elina started getting a lot of pimples on her face. She never had issues with milk, no lactose intolerance or anything. She took care of her skin for years but it was a constant struggle.

In Feb 2019, we learnt about how milk can be damaging to human beings in a 7 day conference in Fiji.

Despite loving it so much and used to having it thrice a day, Elina completely stopped milk in late Feb and within 2.5 months, the magic happened! She was awarded with a clear glowing skin – something that she had wanted for years!

Someone could argue there was something else but this isn't a discussion about milk.

It is about what is possible **if you are willing to look beyond the things that you know**. Milk was such a part of our family habits, that barring aside a medical condition such as Lactose intolerance, there was no reason ever to challenge it!

3 reasons why we gained this massive result for Elina:

- Exposure to new information

- Challenging ourselves and starting new

- Sticking with the new long enough to make it a habit

Nothing would have happened, if we had just "tried" for a while and not gone all the way. In fact, if we had left it in 2 months, our long-held beliefs would have further been affirmed – wouldn't have been correct though!

Belief and continuous non-stop actions lead to success.

"Non-stop focused action leads to results"

You can change the focus – if something isn't working out.

Start with an objective, take action, adjust based on results, again take actions and persist till you get the intended objective.

It is that simple. What results you want will come from focused consistent actions.

Let us consider another key element of the building block.

TRIANGLE OF LIFE – FOCUS ON HOW?

"To be yourself in a world that is constantly trying to make you something else is the greatest accomplishment."

– Ralph Waldo Emerson

Let us focus on how you want to be in your life. With a million choices to focus on, how can we narrow it down to some basic needs as individuals.

Your individuality is what matters most; however, this is often misunderstood as being a lone wolf, who is standing against the tides. Some take it as a rebel, some see it as a set of behaviour and style one must develop and some are massively misguided as they see it as being a winner at all times.

Individuality is sacred in the sense that without an individual, there is no sense in a collective.

Even with that clarity, too many people compromise with one or more aspects of life because going after things that give us wealth, is the quickest way to feel as if we are progressing.

The triangle of life is designed from our guiding philosophy of life;

"Each human being is born to stand tall, have energy and vitality- in mind, body and spirit and have a strong hold on his triangle of life- Achievements, Health and Relationships"

– Shilpa and Kapil

The concept "Triangle of Life' is designed to ensure that each of us give due attention to the critical aspects in our life.

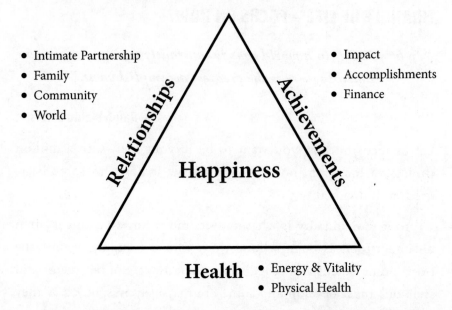

- Intimate Partnership
- Family
- Community
- World

- Impact
- Accomplishments
- Finance

Relationships

Achievements

Happiness

Health
- Energy & Vitality
- Physical Health

The 3 elements- Achievements, Health and Relationships have to be in synch for any individual. Any lack of coherence in terms of focus across these 3 areas, will lead to significant issues and is bound to create a disbalance that each of us would want to avoid.

Health and Relationship aspects need to be built slowly. They are the ones that need most care – not by sheer force but by nurturing them consistently every day.

Achievement segment is a brute force segment – you put a lot of focus on it and you can get a good output in a short time. However, it can be extremely limiting, sometimes, as most people focus majority of their time and energy on this segment and somehow balance the other aspects with, "when the time is right".

Let us do a quick thought experiment. Think of at least one thing that you did that didn't serve you well in life.

It is likely that this was related to decisions in Health or

Relationships. These two have to be in alignment with the third segment of Achievement or your life would hold little meaning.

Still, you made that choice – because it seemed like a smart thing to do at that time. In all likelihood, you did not have a choice and you were driven by the older, reactionary way.

> *"Life has to be BUILT, not barely LIVED"*

> **- Shilpa K**

The Triangle of Life is how it comes together for each one of us.

It is how you want to BE in life across the 3 areas, that encapsulate everything that is important and is part of being human. Growth and happiness are possible only if each arm of the triangle grows in coherence with other arms.

Let us now look into each of these independently, how they impact us and how we must take care of them.

Relationships

No matter what background you have, the core of your existence is about who loves you, engages with you and who you love and engage with. Yet, managing relationships are mostly something we learn as we go through life.

Unfortunately, most of us pretend to be experts at it, yet suck at it badly as we jump into one pothole after another. Some even consider it necessary to do that – as a crucial experience to have, so that they can deserve the best later on.

A number of years back, we were part of a Hindu house warming ceremony. The priest was an Aussie, who was well versed with

Hindu practices. He shared something that beautifully combined the eastern and western philosophy of self and irrespective of your faith, will appeal to you.

As per that, there are 4 level of relationships.

Level 1- Relationship with yourself - who you are, how do you see yourself? When you look in the mirror, who do you see?

You have to first take care of yourself before you can help others.

Even in the aeroplane, the crew always says that during an emergency, first put your own mask and then make other people wear it.

Level two is your relationship with your family & close friends - people who are around you, in your inner circle. These are the people who are dependent on you or you are on them.

The idea is, take care of those who are close to you.

Level 3 is your relationship with your community - These are the people who are part of your social environment, workplace, your vicinity and all those communities that you are part of.

The idea here is to contribute to your social surroundings.

Level four is your relationship with humanity – This covers how you contribute to humanity as a whole.

Each of us have an inherent desire to find a bigger meaning in life. It may be in the form of leaving a legacy or giving value to people. It is one of the highest expressions of ourselves.

On a completely opposite spectrum, there are people, who talk as if their life is all about other people and they are self-sabotaging their own happiness for the sake of other people. These people are either faking it or not articulating it well, but they get stuck in this idea that it is somehow sinful to consider oneself at the centre of existence.

In the movie Titanic, Jack Dawson dies while leaving Rose on the broken door to help her survive the aftermath of the Titanic going down. Many people consider that it was Jack's sacrifice to save Rose. Let us consider this and remove any conflict with the above.

The dictionary meaning of "Sacrifice" is "give up (something valued) for the sake of other considerations."

If this thing that is "given up", has a **higher value** for you as an individual, would you give it up in exchange of a lower value?

If you were on Titanic and it was an option between you and your child, who would you have chosen? Her/his life carry a higher value as you would not be able to live in the world, where such choices constrain your hand.

You would jump off that door, if it means letting your child live. This is not a sacrifice. This is an act of absolute self-love. You are taking care of your own sanity.

Those who consider that they are sacrificing for others create a regular pattern in their life, where the only end result is victimhood.

"I did so much for them and this is what they did!"

You have to focus on yourself first. This is not to say that you become self-centred and stop regarding other people. You cannot exist in isolation of your environment. The way you are important for yourself, the other person's Self also matters.

Understanding this relationship with yourself then creates space to engage with others from the position of strength.

Would you rely on a beggar on the street to give you any money?

A weak person or a person who does not take care of himself CANNOT take care of others.

"To hold one's own life as one's ultimate value, and one's own happiness as one's highest purpose are two aspects of the same achievement."

– Ayn Rand

While you intellectually try to understand and assimilate that knowledge, take this as a core principle.

You cannot be successful without a complete belief that you have to put yourself in the centre of your life and create a space for projecting it out to other people with whatever purpose you want to live with.

Health

"One Day or Day one – You Decide"

- Shilpa K

Few years back, we saw a "motivational" talk from one of gurus, who was talking about the importance of health, eating right and living life well. The talk was really good.

The only problem was, the Guru himself had a huge belly.

It was funny in a way. Wait! It gets better!

There are coaches across the world, who are talking about mindset transformation yet are themselves rather unfit. How can anyone in their sane mind consider these coaches as credible people to learn from, if they cannot themselves take care of their health?

The Crew Director of one of the most popular personal development events in the world, is in the personal development industry for 25 years, is amazingly brilliant and organised but is really unfit physically with a really large belly.

We are not doing fat shaming here – but barring aside some medical challenges that people have, a fat human body cannot be considered healthy. Each of these extraordinarily accomplished individuals have a shorter lifespan just because they are not playing it full in the Health Aspect of their life. It will catch up with them eventually.

Your one life – your need to play it full – it is not worth anything unless you have a health to enjoy it as well!

The first component of Health is your **Physical Health**.

If we put aside people who have physical disabilities, or those with diseases that has some impact on their weight, normal people do not have an excuse for being horizontally challenged, or to put it plainly, fat and unhealthy!

Human being didn't evolve to be such. Our ancestors were nimble on their feet, quick and strong. Fat storage became a mechanism that evolved to keep stock for the hard time, which was inevitable for that hard life they lived.

We do not belong in that era. We don't have to keep an extra stock of fat in our body any longer. Eating a lot is an evolutionary mechanism and if there is one common thread throughout the book that you must get, it is about YOUR ONE LIFE – where you have to play it full at all levels across all areas of the Triangle of Life.

Being fat and unhealthy is about being not in control of what you feed your body. It is a simple equation. People relate losing weight to exercise but that is only 10% of it, 90% of it is what you eat.

And if someone as intelligent as you, as committed as you and as charged up as you, does not have control on what you eat – it has to have an impact on whatever else you want to do in life.

You may wonder why is it important?

"How you show up for small things is how you show up for big things as well"

If you are not fit, strong, whatever you will accomplish, contribute or whatever relationships you have will be short lived because unfortunately, your life could be cut short. Hard but true.

You MUST take care of your health.

The other component of Health is your **Energy & Vitality**. Your energy makes you a magnet that repels or attract people, success, wealth – everything that you want.

For instance, you cannot have huge amount of success with a low energy level. **It is not possible**. How you appear in small things is how you appear in big things. It just becomes second nature and before you know it, you are acting like that everywhere.

In fact, you can test it right now!

Get up right now (unless you are in a place you cannot- example driving or in office) and shake your whole body, do 20-star jumps.

Come on do it... pull yourself up.

20 Star jumps...GO!

Now that you have done it, you can yourself see that you feel much better and you will have much better focus.

We are definitely under a delusion that reading this book must be making you feel great. However definitely the star jumps will help you see how easy it is, at any point of time, for you to get energised!

Achievements

The third part of the triangle is Achievements. This is incidentally why you probably picked up this book.

The challenge that most people face is that they consider this as **the most important** part. But we will come back to that later.

For now, the **first component** of Achievement is **"Impact"**.

What impact you are making in the environment where you work? What value you are creating?

"The only way to earn money is take something from Disorganised state to Organized state by adding Value."

- Benjamin J Harvey

This is what businesses across the world do. That is how they generate wealth.

Whether you are in business or in job, your achievements are about the **Impact you make by generating value**.

Second component of Achievement segment is **"Accomplishment"**.

What you accomplish in life gives you a sense of achievement.

Ask yourself: What results you are producing that are noticed by other people and appreciated?

You continuously want to repeat those as it helps you get a powerful personal brand, develop a strong sense of worth and feeds into building your financial muscles.

The accomplishments often result in the titles/designations and there is often significant respect associated with that.

"Your accomplishments mean that you are worth listening to"

– John Pittard

The third component of Achievement segment is **"Financial"**. This is the money you are making with all the efforts you put in.

The entire ethical & commercial construct of personal power is around building your wealth by creating value in whatever you do.

If you make money by creating value – it is a great thing to have. It allows you freedom, it allows you to take care of your other needs. Bring Money in coherence with who you are and see the magic created in your life!

The Triangle of Life describes the essence of how you want TO BE in life. Far too many people focus on making only one side of the triangle bigger. You can probably see, why this wouldn't work! The distorted triangle is one thing but one of the sides being bigger means, a certain oddity in life– which symbolises chaos!

Your job is to play it full by focusing on all the three areas. The more you do, the bigger your triangle becomes- which simply means growth as a human being.

A bigger triangle with the length of each side symbolizes the extent of your focus and reward in each. The happiness is at the centre of this triangle and is related to your growth across all the 3 areas.

THE EXECUTION PRINCIPLES – 4 PILLARS – FOCUS ON WHAT?

The Triangle of Life covers how you want to be across various areas in life. However, as we have seen in previous sections, understanding something intellectually is not sufficient for success.

What will guide you to that path?

The 4 pillars- Beliefs, Purpose, Standards and Actions, create a strong foundation for you to build a life of purpose and play it full.

Pillar 1 – Beliefs

> *"The only boundaries to success are our own boundaries of belief"*
>
> **– Brandon Burchard**

Kapil: A Transition to Luck

When I was in year 12, the trend was for everyone to appear in engineering entrance exams to get into the best possible engineering college. As a middle-class family, this was the biggest aspiration, my parents had from me and my twin. This was our ticket out to affluence.

Both me and my twin worked hard at it, burning midnight oil. We had standard Physics, Chemistry and Maths as the subject we had to master. Wanting to get into the premier institutes (IIT) in India was a huge driver for us.

I loved maths, tolerated chemistry and looked at physics with wonder and incomprehension. I still remember going through

---

the bible of physics - Resnick Halliday's part 2, which covered rotational motion that I just couldn't get!

My other challenge was having a rather fixation with doing only those things that I love and the single mindedness with which I went after things that I loved doing.

"When you have maths, why would you do physics" – I would say to anyone who would listen to a 17 year' old boy!

Post the IIT exam (which is aimed to get admission in Indian Institute of Technology, which are internationally recognised educational institutes and produce high quality scientists, engineers and technologists), I knew I won't make it and my twin knew he will as he had nailed the exam (later at the results time, he got 230th rank across all India, which was quite cool).

One of the things, twins possess in abundance is competing with each other- in a positive way! After failing first time, I decided to dedicate my next one year to IIT entrance exam and decided to skip other engineering entrance exams coming up in a month, almost considering them beneath me!

My dad saw what was coming and told my twin to continue to study for the upcoming Pre-Engineering Test (PET) for other good college, a rung lower than IIT, despite having certainty that he will make it to IIT.

Seeing him continuing to study for the PET, I followed him and it was a saving grace. I did well. However, it didn't matter – I had decided to drop the year and prepare for the highly sought after IIT entrance exam next year.

Where am I going with it? This was going to create one of the most damaging belief, I was getting into – so read on!

In less than 2 months, I mastered the dreaded physics! Rotational motion was right there on my fingertips. I had fallen in love with science!

When the PET result came, I had scored a home run and as per the wisdom of middle class, "don't leave what you have in your hand for what may or may not come" – I dropped the idea of IIT and entered one of the other prestigious regional engineering college.

But the damage was done.

My mastering Resnick Halliday's rotational physics came at a very heavy cost, that was to define a large part of my life.

A limited belief, "I am one year too early for everything" started, creating a series of self-damaging and limiting behaviours that had heavy consequences across all aspects of my life.

Even getting into PET wasn't spared! "I got lucky" seeped in my consciousness and when I connected the dots, it seems to be the way life had turned out till then!

Steve Jobs once said, you can only connect the dots looking backward. What he missed saying though is, it is a conscious, thought through process. Otherwise, what it results into is a distorted version of your personal reality.

My two beliefs, "I am one year too early for everything" and "I get lucky", went on to drive a lot of my life for next 28 years!

Your beliefs have significantly more control of your life than you realise it! You will always act in accordance with your beliefs.

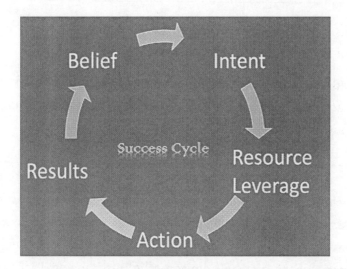

The below cycle of Belief-Intent-Resource Leverage-Action-Results (BILAR) cycle explains this really well.

Let us say that you have a belief that your communication is bad. It may have developed over time because of various inputs you got from your parents, friends, relatives, teachers and bosses.

Suppose you get an opportunity to make a presentation to your CEO, who is visiting your location.

You have a clear result and direction, yet despite having the best intentions, just because your belief is that you have communication issues, you will approach it with an **intent to NOT do a bad job**. Of course, you will never say it out loud but every part in your body will focus on things **not going wrong**.

You would then leverage the resources around you to get that action and result. If you have that intent of NOT doing a bad job (with a focus on *NOT*), you will end up **under leveraging** all the resources you have available.

That would mean that your actions will be half hearted.

This would produce average results that will affirm the belief you had about your communication being bad.

Read the above once again, if you are taken aback. We always act in accordance with our beliefs, which build a self-image and that's how we show up.

Kapil: A friend of mine battled weight loss for years. Once I lost my weight, which he encouraged and gave a lot of great input to (he had a great intellectual knowledge on the subject), he was inspired in his own way to start the process. He engaged a dietician, whose diet he followed religiously losing 12 KG in 6 months, which was fantastic.

I saw him loving his salads and the food that he prepared with great delight. He really kept the temptation of the unhealthy food away. He started gym and was basking in the glory of his newly found happiness.

Yet, within 6-8 months, his weight- loss hit a plateau, much before his goal of ideal weight and he started gaining it back bit by bit.

However much, I wanted to contribute, he resisted those discussions due to my style of challenging his beliefs and his style being focused on knowledge. The resistance was constant, despite visible indication of gradual weight increase.

I don't know how will it be in years to come – but it is sad that he allowed himself to be part of a statistics as to how most people who diet and lose weight, go back within a short period of time.

Weight loss is about Self Image. I sustained easily without effort for years, because, my relationship with food changed and I got into a positive BILAR cycle.

People who win the war with their weight forever not only change their relationship with food but also bring a significant change in the **way they view themselves.** They change their belief about themselves and the things in their environment.

"The only way to beat temptation is to not have it."

– Kapil K

We have to create new associations in our mind about the things we want to avoid but can't because of the battle that goes on in our little head and holds us back.

Shilpa: Years back I lost my beloved dad, at a young age of 55 due to a massive heart attack. As someone in early twenties, I just couldn't comprehend why that happened only to me, while my other friends kept holidaying with their dads happily, for endless years thereafter.

But there was one thing that happened – losing him hit me with a huge repulsion to the food habits in our family – oily parathas, vegetables loaded with ghee and other fried stuff that we had on a daily basis. I knew that these food habits played a massive role in my family losing the brightest light of our lives.

And then it happened – it just took a moment – for me to switch my relationship with food. I consciously developed a relationship of pain with that oily, fried food and I started associating a lot of pleasure with fresh fruits, colourful vegetables and crunchy nuts.

20 years hence and my relationship with food has stayed the same.

I cannot help but smile when people feel that I am depriving myself of the tasty stuff. I never do.

It is not that I never eat junk, I do. However, it is a conscious choice to decide when and whether it is worth the calories. Because I associate much pleasure with "Healthy food" and an unbearable pain with "Unhealthy food", these occasions are far and few.

I never struggle with temptations – never.

I have taken it to the core of my belief system, which affects my intent, my leverage, actions and my results.

Too many of the great changes and fantastic results are dead because of that statement that you have told yourself through the years.

"Our success is a result of our beliefs and our beliefs are fed by our success"

– Shilpa K

The way to break this chicken and egg story is to start with empowering beliefs (covered in the next chapter)

One of the most significant beliefs that has taken a new meaning in this connected global work place and market is "Abundance".

A lot has been written about the Abundance mindset but we want to share a highly relevant "cannot-ignore" idea around abundance, that is absolutely essential for an extraordinary life.

It is not possible to fake this mindset – it has to be developed in your gut!

You really need to believe it and it has to become a core of who you truly are. For that, let us get some challenges out of the way.

Do you go by the myth that you can have an abundance mindset only when you have enough? It is actually the other way around. Only when you develop this mindset, can you achieve "enough". When you start with that premise, you start engaging with people differently, which in turn creates completely unexpected opportunities.

All of us have been in a situation, where something someone said, created a flood of ideas. That is possible only, when people share without any fear of loss of their IP.

Shilpa: Years back, when I was working for Westpac, a Business Analyst joined my team. This person had been in quite senior positions earlier and had worked for some large companies, in another country. However, he was totally new to the project space and this side of the world.

On the first day of his job, I found him sitting after-hours struggling with some process maps. Back then, I was a process expert, so I told him to go home and promised to help him with the process design for the Business Unit, that he was entrusted with.

I sat down with him daily, intermittently with my day job and within a week, he developed incredibly well, and to be honest, a much better expert than I was.

I got an "Outstanding" rating that year. But that is not my point here. To get the real juice of this true story, read on.

He with a lot of open-mindedness, took it as the way of life" and he started portraying a similar behaviour to the other people in the team.

> Soon this concept of free sharing, no holding back became a norm and people from our portfolio became highly sought-after candidates by the other portfolios, who were keen to inherit a similar abundance mentality.

Abundance is a beautiful concept. When you know that other's success is not at the cost of yours and lifting others is a part of lifting yourself as well, the feeling that there is enough for everyone can go on to change this world.

That said, there are many people who still closely guard their secrets. A lot of our clients have a concern – if I give it away, someone can copy it.

Yes, they can copy it in their own way, with their own interpretation of what they think the solution should be. But they cannot duplicate your uniqueness, your enthusiasm, your style and how you perceive the solution to be.

There may be further doubts that if you give away the solution, isn't that everything?

No, because in today's fast-moving world, your solution WILL necessarily change as you go forward, talk to people, work on it and take it to market.

If you hold it to yourself, you can only take it only so far – within YOUR limits. But if you engage others, the idea can grow exponentially-it can form communities who build on top of each other. This will take the game higher, to gift this world with a 10X better solution and make a much larger impact.

Shilpa: In my daughter's 18th birthday party, she invited one of her old friends, whom we had last seen 10 years back. As we talked, she showed me photos of a table she designed and a series of IQ lamps that she had created. When I asked her about why she is not selling it on ebay – she admitted that she was concerned about someone copying it.

In a very short discussion, she understood the idea of applying the Abundance principle and understood that while people can copy a design, they can hardly ever get it implemented. Even if they do, it doesn't impact her as by sharing more, she will be able to tap into the market place in a very unique way as an expert, who has enough so that others can learn from her.

It is possible and probable that if you share your ideas openly, those will be copied. But isn't that that a validation of a great idea? It is worth something to someone. And once you put yourself out there, you will expose yourself to a lot more to build on, and the traction you will get will be incomparable.

Benjamin J Harvey and Chang Tam of Authentic Education Australia lay it out bare for their participants in the course "Difference Maker Accelerator" and "Present like a Pro", that they are happy for people to take anything out of the course material and use it as long as they either gave Authentic Education a credit or use the concept, with some changes in the representation.

That is an amazing display of abundance mindset. We wouldn't expect them to put this course online free of course but letting other coaches grow and leverage their learning is how they conceptually think. For them it is not an issue because they are driven by their mission to enable coaches to grow their impact and income.

Sharing, with abundance at the core, is a great strategy for growth. It gets you noticed. It establishes you as an expert. It makes people believe in you.

You have to believe that your ideas will never dry. You have to believe that your capability will never be reduced and you will continue to be ahead of anyone, simply because people can copy your ideas but they cannot take your uniqueness away.

Abundance mindset removes the negative competition out of the way and creates exponential growth possible.

Pillar 2 – Purpose & Goals

"Great minds have purpose; others have wishes"

– Washington Irving

As you saw in earlier part of the book, majority of your life has been on autopilot with an illusion of control in your hand. Most of the amazing things you have achieved are often accomplished while responding to external situations. Playing it full in life is about making conscious choices and taking the control in your hands, to consciously create wins all along.

What bridges that gap between your internal power and the results you achieve, is actually the direction your life takes. Too many people live their life, just going around and round in motion with few nudges from external situations that sends them moving slightly forward but their lives do not hold much meaning.

A majority of people then become satisfied with engineering smallness in their lives.

The question is, how beautiful, powerful, strong, energetic life is and what you do with it.

There are 2 key reasons why having a purpose changes your game and elevates your level in life.

One, it allows you to enable others and give your own existence a deeper meaning

Two, people with purpose are 4-5 times more likely to succeed in wealth, health and relationships.

Whichever one appeals to you! We are yet to meet people who do not want both. The first one is a "pleasure response", the second one is a "pain/pleasure" response depending on how you read it.

Your purpose in life gives you a power beyond anything you currently can imagine.

What is purpose?

It is what you make it to be – **the key component of purpose is contribution**. Great thing about this is, there is no comparison to those before you and those will come after you. You are on the planet earth and you need to find out yourself what you can contribute.

The bigger the game you play, the bigger will be your contribution!

"It's clear that the days of 'engineering smallness and playing it safe to avoid criticism' are over"

– Brene` Brown

How do you find your purpose?

The process of finding your purpose is described in next chapter. An important element of this is that purpose is not a small matter and you don't want to get desperate at finding it. At the least, it mustn't create a feeling of despondency, otherwise it will definitely result in inaction.

It is like dating. You don't finalise this is the person for you on the first date. You date a few people over time and then when you feel it is right, you decide if he/she is for you.

Purpose is like that.

You identify it based on what gives you true happiness, freedom and a sense of growth. You also hopefully have a sense that there is wealth and financial freedom in chasing that and ensure that your beliefs are in alignment. And then you start dating it. You start talking to people about it and if all goes well, **you get obsessed with it!**

If in the early stages, talking about it leaves you exhausted, it isn't your purpose. If it leaves you exasperated, or exhilarated – well, you may have just found your purpose!

Exasperation means, you feel the urge to change something. Exhilaration means, you can do it for free and it will be an amazing thing to be paid for that as well!

This pillar of Purpose & Goals is absolutely critical as it provides your life a direction. If you do not have a direction, whatever you do will not be as effective. It would be like shooting darts in whichever direction you feel like and then being happy when one of them hits somewhere.

Some people are happy with that. The fact you are reading it, means you are not happy with this trial and error approach.

Pillar 3 – Standards

"If you don't set a baseline standard for what you'll accept in life, you'll find it's easy to slip into behaviours and attitudes or a quality of life that's far below what you deserve."

– Tony Robbins

One of the most critical components of walking on the purpose and accomplishing those goals is to have standards in life. Standards means the level you decide for things to be at, at the least if not better.

If you do not have these bars or if you have but you do not follow, no one would know except you.

Kapil: A number of years back, I had a subcontractor, Priya at Microsoft from one of their SI partners in my team. She switched to a full-time job with another SI partner as the first one wasn't giving her a full-time employment.

As her manager, I had informed about this change to my manager and also to Microsoft Vendor Manager and got their go ahead.

All the boxes were ticked.

As soon as she was seen back in my team, the first SI partner (which was employing her as a contractor) complained to the Vendor Manager and soon the issue got escalated to the Microsoft India head and I, my manager and the Vendor Manager was ushered into the meeting with the GM for India operation.

The GM started the meeting with a clear statement that Priya must be asked to leave as we cannot keep unethical people in the team.

The Vendor Manager for some odd reason decided to throw this person under the bus. In reality, she had made a mistake by approving my request that it was ok for Priya to switch jobs from one SI to another SI and still remain at Microsoft.

My manager Tarun just left the decision of what I say and do to me. It was supposedly a tough call! On one hand, I had an influential vendor manager and on another, the right thing to do. I chose the right thing to do without hesitation and Tarun supported me fully.

Priya stayed in that team for another year and that vendor manager became one of the most uncooperative persons I ever worked with.

I didn't do it for Priya. She would have never known what happened, if she was asked to leave and it was easy for me to gain favours and strengthen my relationship with a "powerful" person.

My standards saved the day for me. It wasn't a tough call to make.

While no one else would have really cared about the choice I made, I wouldn't have been the man I am, unless I consistently operated by my standards.

You may recall the story of how I got into Microsoft – that interview at late night when I **refused to give up**. What I didn't know then, the reason for that performance was simpler than I realised.

My standards drove me to do what **I thought was the only option**. The choices I made weren't made in isolation or as a random response to a situation.

There was a pattern- a code that I have followed.

This book is an effort to introduce the code to others and allow them to discover their own standards to help them stand apart and start playing it full.

Standards are like this big block of concrete we stand on our entire life. Far too many times, some good opportunity comes along that needs us to accommodate, adjust **only a bit** and we can win the day. Many times, our existing constraints come in, or our financial challenges crop up, or something happens and **we adjust a bit, only a bit**!

Those are the times a crack gets introduced that we don't even notice.

It is a long life – things keep coming up. Newer, smaller or bigger cracks keep appearing and we keep standing.

Till few of those come together to shake our foundations.

Standards are THAT important. They are different from rules that are created by other people and are meant to be followed by us OR broken by us.

Standards are created by us, only for us!

Shilpa: My father once told me a story of this shoe cobbler (Called 'Mochi" in Hindi) in India. Dad used to get his shoes fixed from this roadside person since about 15 years. Once they got talking and this Mochi told him that he has a big 3 floor house and one of his sons is a doctor and one is an engineer. Appalled, my dad asked him, why does he work here on the road side?

The Mochi said, "Sir this work is the reason, why that happened. This is work and work is worship. If I stop this, nothing I have done has any value".

That was his standard in practice!

Lot of people wonder what is the key to being successful. If you read about successful people and their struggles, success didn't come because they were addicted to success –**they were actually addicted to standards.**

We all know about the rocket-man, Elon Musk. He is lives as per his own standards.

We know about Richard Branson, the maverick, the genius and a man with simplicity and difference. He is addicted to standards and he doesn't let the age/gender/nationality/past difference come between him and his standards.

Standards in life are defined by YOURSELF, AT YOUR WILL, AT YOUR LEISURE, FOR YOUR LIFE, NEVER to be compromised.

"Your success is about the standards you set for yourself."

– Kapil K

This is one of the biggest game-changer.

Consider some of your best accomplishments– did they just happen to fall in your lap or you worked for it?

They were your standards. You don't have to define them afresh; you have to just identify them, align them to your goals and raise them higher!

Pillar 4 – Action

"We are not sum of our intentions but of our Actions"

– Brandon Burchard

Shilpa: In Grant Cardone's 10X bootcamp in Sydney, one of the attendees asked Grant for his investment in an amazing $1 Trillion idea over next 10 years – he even shared the calculation.

127,000 businesses will buy it and pay $2000 per day for it. That is about $927 Billion in 10 years.

What a deal!

Grant said, "how many have your sold".

"None, but I am about done with the product" the guy explained.

"How long have you been working on it", Grant asked

"2 years, but it is a revolutionary product", quipped the person.

"Well, sell the first one and then come back to me", with that, Grant said to the rest of the audience, "there is always someone, who has a massive idea, no execution and thinks that he is changing the world".

"A mountain of wealth is hiding under rubble of inaction"

– Kapil K

Without action, anything you plan is useless!

If you have a strong set of beliefs, a goal and your standards set up, action is not difficult since you are driven to succeed.

However, there is a difference in the action that gets you result and action that keep you going in circles. In the example above with Grant Cardone, the individual in question probably had the first three pillars defined but didn't really take massive actions.

Massive action does not mean BIG actions. It means series of forward moving consistent actions that are aligned with the direction you are taking.

Why?

Because the only way to get something done is to **actually do it,** test if it works, course correct it and keep at it till you get it done!

Sometimes, you meet people who are just incredible and you can see the fire and their clarity oozing through every word they say. Yet, a little deep into the conversation, you see that, they have been working on that fantastic idea or project since ages. They are brilliant but their lack of execution discipline is not letting that brilliance be visible to the rest of the world.

You meet them some years later, and you are likely to see them at the status quo.

We all have friends, who have been planning to open business since years but are caught up in the 9-to-5 loop. They get too tired on weekdays to hustle after office and are too busy on weekends with their parties and "charging up".

We all have also known people, who are amazing at what they do, earn good money but are very dissatisfied in their lives.

In our own journey as well, we have seen enough to confirm that it all boils down to one single differentiating factor- ACTION!

"Action is the key that unlocks your potential."

– Shilpa K

To get into the right mindset and accomplish great things - we need to get right three foundational elements- Physiology, Focus and Language.

The first key element is Physiology.

Having the right physiology is so critical that almost everything you will ever accomplish is associated with that.

Shilpa: Once Kapil and I were going to the Sydney CBD in a train and I got upset with him for something – I remember feeling helpless and anger washing all over my face. Kapil told me about Asstitude –Joseph Mcclendon's amazing principle!

He told me to do it. What? Shake that ass? In train? In public? I was petrified and obviously I was even more angry! But he and I have a pact that we will do it – the moment we are asked. I was determined that I am angry and shaking my bum is not going to do anything.

Well – I did that while sitting and next thing I know, I just couldn't help but smile!

My physiology changed – my state became positive.

Your physiology is VERY powerful – you can literally change your mood, how you feel by changing your physiology.

The second critical element is Focus.

Consider any accomplishments in your life –you would find that you were not only in control of yourself, your physiology but also, you had a die-hard commitment to whatever cause you were chasing.

You almost had single minded FOCUS on what you were doing.

Success was easy – whatever area of life it was.

It is applicable to family life as well. For those who are parents – you can relate that it isn't difficult to love your children – you have no doubt about what kind of relationship you are going to have with them.

Some of you may ponder – why am I relating "no doubt" with focus. It is deeply connected. When you are focused on something – your action is so massive that you move with the speed and ferociousness of a tiger – without any doubts about the validity of what you are doing.

If you focus on your health, your relationships, your work – there is no way, it wouldn't lead to massive results.

"Energy does Flow Where Focus Goes"

– Tony Robbins

Where you start focusing your attention, that is where your energy flows and that is where you get your accomplishments come from.

The third triad is Language – This has been revolutionary for us personally. Just by changing what words we speak, there has been a significant shift in our life.

The basic emotions in human mind are controlled by our Amygdala – our hind brain – or our animal brain. That is the stem behind our head and is designed to keep us safe. The right and left portions of the amygdala have independent memory systems, but work together to store, encode, and interpret emotion.

The right hemisphere is associated with negative emotion. For instance, fear. We are biologically hardwired to express them. Controlling them is always a challenge.

As a matter of fact, changing your physiology can actually make a difference to these emotions. For instance, when you are fearful, you can stand tall, put both your hands on your waist and make loud gestures – you will see fear disappearing.

Assume a situation -

You suddenly feel anger for your partner doing something you don't want him or her to do

If you were to use language in your head such as "Oh, she/he is causing all this trouble" – would your anger increase?

If you were to use language such as "I am not really angry" – would your anger become more controllable?

We create reality with our language. What we say can massively change our circumstances. A self-pep talk before a critical presentation can go a much longer way than watching a motivational youtube video.

Even what you allow that little voice in your head to say can make a big difference to how actually act. When going after a goal, if you say something positive – but internally allow that little voice to use negative words, you will automatically reduce the effort and make it really difficult.

Shilpa: One of my mentees had a significant confidence challenge and soon, I could see that he was constantly using negative words to beat himself up. The often-repeated sentence was "I am not that intelligent".

On being challenged in one of the sessions, in just next week, his language changed. It has been 2 months since then and he has never once used it – even when he is in full flow, expressing himself. His life has taken such a big turn as his eyes are now turned to big goals – that he considered impossible before!

Your language is very powerful, so use it carefully. It can literally make you successful or destroy it.

To check your language, take a break right now and talk to your partner or a close friend. Ask them, what is the most repeated negative words you use for yourself.

Write all of them on a page in LARGE CAPITAL LETTERS – really large and LOUD.

Now take that paper. Fold it neatly in two.

Tear it with Violence. With a loud gesture – be as dramatic as you can be. Throw it in a bin with contempt and anger and drama!

There it is – GONE! Forever.

You are not going to allow that crap to define who you are. You are not going to allow that to demean you any further. You are NOT that person anymore. It doesn't matter what you did. You are NOT that person anymore.

Let us now review how far we have come and what the next section covers."

Chapter 1 covered about how do we do things currently and what is the issue with that. This chapter helped you develop an understanding of your motivations and how you operate.

Chapter 2 covered about WHY of what we do. We looked into our deep-rooted beliefs and reasons of the specific way we operate. Here we also looked into the self-imposed obstacles and how they impact our decisions in life.

Chapter 3 covered the key solution components that create building blocks for a powerful career. An understanding of them now has given you a deep awareness of how to take your career to next level.

====

Chapter 4 contains the solution based on our 7-step process and key how it needs to be executed in your life. Now you are ready to absorb this and implement it in your life.

PART 3

Chapter 4
The Path to Fast Career Growth

"Challenge yourself. It is the only path which leads to growth"

– **Morgan Freeman**

Now that you have a deep intellectual understanding about what holds you back in life and the building blocks you need to put in place, let us get into the details of the exact path you can take in your life.

This path will bring a fundamental shift in your mindset and you will regain the same fire you once had as a 19-year-old, who was ready to conquer this world.

One question that comes up when we start coaching people – especially in the first session is, what has my career got to do with these steps, most of which are inside-out not outside-in?

The reason is that instead of focussing on short-term tactics and behaviours, we enable fundamental shifts inside you. We are sharing secrets that have worked wonders for our mentees, enabling them to create outstanding lives, in the area of their choice and this will give you the ammunition to live powerfully, in a sustainable manner.

Most people know Robbin Williams. He was one of the best comedians, an enterprising individual and well respected in the movie industry for 20 years!

In early days, he decided to have his own television show. He was the first comedian to do it! Then he wanted to make a movie – he did that as well! Then wanted to make a serious movie – he got an Oscar for that!

Anything that he touched turned into gold!

He decided to do a solo tour of 26 cities, something no other comedian had done before and again, he was super successful.

Despite these achievements, he committed suicide in 2014 – driven by manic depression. The main cause was Parkinson's disease and paranoia. And amidst all this, he had also abused his body really badly – drugs, alcohol, etc.

Working towards fulfilling life and career is NOT a luxury or a dream. It is the NEED of the hour!

This can make you feel energised, but there remains a significant issue of **charting the path and actually walking on it.**

Most people think that their life is divided in 2 parts and their whole concentration is on creating a balance between the two.

A close friend brings this to every discussion as to how he has an ability to switch off a part of his brain when he leaves office and how he can actually neatly divide his life in two clean parts- one professional and one personal.

If you are like that, it is time to get rid of those beliefs. We can assure you. Your progress will be awfully slow, if you have this split personality.

You have one life- one mind and only one personality!

How you show at work is how you show at home as well.

In fact, any delusion related to it can be broken if you just interview 5 people from work place and 5 from your personal setting. You will find that you have one single style of who you are.

"Yes, that must be true – still I can switch myself off" some of you may argue.

Let us test it by considering the extreme case. You may skip next few lines, if you already agree that you have ONE life!

If your kid is unwell, quite unwell, can you focus on work and produce the same result as you would if everything in life was good?

If your project is going very bad and you are held responsible for the significant challenges, would you be able to come home and spend quality time with your family?

I doubt if anyone can say Yes to both or any of these.

But the doubts still linger. Right? We have only considered extremities. Let us build on this further.

Sachin Tendulkar, one of the world's finest batsman, decided to come to the crease for his team during the world cup in 1999, despite getting the news that his father passed away.

To others, it seems Sachin was able to keep things separate. If they dig deep however, they will find, that there was never a dichotomy in his mind. The game was his best expression of himself.

He obviously used his mental muscles to control his emotions and pain but that doesn't mean he switched off a part of his personality. In reality, he actually stayed one, where most people will fall apart!

Sachin shared in his book "Playing It My Way" that his mind wasn't always in the game but he dedicated the century to his father as "he would have wanted me to play".

(Side note: Sachin also picked up his famous habit of looking to heavens after every century – as if to celebrate his father's ever-present love.)

Let us build on these extremes and the above example. Our interactions with our environment, our actions and our reactions depend on our beliefs, values, standards and other deep part of our psyche that exhibits ONENESS.

Being under the delusion that one can split this ONENESS in two separate parts is ludicrous, delusional and denies us an opportunity to **find our personal power** that we can express under all the circumstances.

You are just one and how you do a small thing is how you do a big thing. Being able to understand yourself deeply and building on that core is the path to personal power and all the riches that come with that.

"You cannot compartmentalize your personal and professional life separately"

– Kapil Kulshreshtha

You are one single person.

Back in early 19th century, Einstein used to say, that there are probably 5 people, who understood the General Theory of Relativity. Now a 16-year-old girl can explain the intricacies better than Einstein.

Everything great emerges out of a creative mind. However, the only way it can be adopted by others is through a simplified structure. The 7-step process is explained below in a structure to help create an overall picture in your mind.

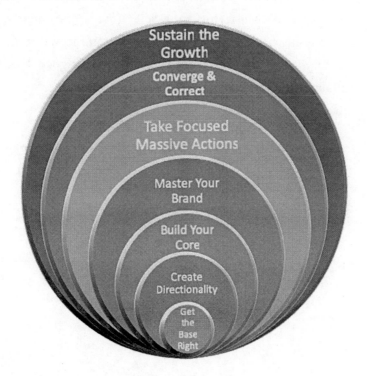

At a high level, this looks fairly straightforward. *Get your base right, Define a Direction, Work on Yourself, Let People know, Actual Massive Execution, Make Corrections and Make it Sustainable.*

Simple!

Not quite. This is not strictly a sequential process. As you are in one stage, the other stage starts – and what you learn as you progress gets firmly embedded in the person you become.

When our mentees walk through this process in our 6 months coaching program, they step through these stages but many elements of the later stages start demanding due attention in between.

For instance, you would start getting some habits for sustenance (Step 7) as part of "Mastering Your Self" (Step 3). Similarly, you would keep going back to the second step as you move through the stages since you continuously need to adjust your goals based on the results you are getting.

As the saying goes, the devil is in the details.

Let us deep dive through the details and see how implementable it is.

STEP 1 – BE AWARE

"Awareness precedes choice and choice precedes results"

– Robin S Sharma

There are long roads in desert in Arizona – with light poles on the side of the road. Invariably when there is an accident, majority of them happen with the cars hitting a pole.

You would think that given that pole would be less than 1% of the entire length, it doesn't make sense!

Human behaviour comes in the way. As a driver loses control, they see the pole and their mind furiously thinks, "Oh no! Anything but the pole" and subconsciously their hands turn the wheel in such a way that it ends up hitting the pole.

Consider your own driving experience – while taking a turn, if you were to look straight, you will find it very difficult to turn the wheel.

What happens?

"Focus goes where energy goes"

– Tony Robbins

If asked, how much do you know yourself, a lot of us will say that we are aware of ourselves 90% of the time - that we know what is awesome about us and what is. wrong with us.

Let us look into that based on age old research and established facts about human behaviour. You may have heard of the classical Johari Window:

	Known to self	Not Known to Self
Known to Others	1 Arena	3 Blind Spot
Not Known to Others	2 Facade	4 Unknown

Qudrant1: Arena: Your visible side to the world

Qudrant2: Façade: This is a façade you have built up, so that others cannot know- whatever is the reason, good or bad.

Qudrant3: Blind Spot: These are like a spot on your forehead that others can see but you can't. These are behaviours so automatic that you do it without even realizing.

Qudrant4: Unknown: These are the things that are hidden gems. When asked, most people will put the 4th segment as very low or almost non-existent.

Typical % splits in each quadrant

Together Quadrant 1 and 2 are about 40% of who you are.

Quadrant 3 is usually about 20% of your overall potential and life.

Quadrant 4 is about 40% or more for a vast majority.

	Known to self	Not Known to Self
Known to Others	Personal Brand 1 Arena	Growth 3 Blind Spot
Not Known to Others	Personal Brand 2 Facade	Transformation 4 Unknown

If you have an inkling that you are very different from people and that you know yourself intimately maybe 90% - consider this - **You don't know what you don't know.** You can either stay in that delusion or use this as an opportunity to transform your life.

Quadrant 1 and 2 together provide a significant opportunity to bring the real you outside. Creating a **personal brand** is the key to then get noticed for who you truly are and start getting opportunities that wouldn't have come otherwise.

Quadrant 3 creates a significant opportunity to know yourself and **grow as an individual**. Most organic, non-transformational growth is pretty much lying under plain sight, if only you talk to people.

Quadrant 4 is something entirely different. We have seen it time and again, when coaching people. In 8-10 weeks of starting with us, most people have an epiphany and previously unexplored and unknown options become widely open!

In fact, in our 30 days Mindset Transformation program, most people get a wide eye within 5 days.

The Segment 4 therefore is the **Transformational Segment.**

Ask yourself the hard questions. Is my health top notch? Are my relations fulfilling and are my achievements / finances up to my standards?

If the answer to any of the above is "No" or a sheepish "Yes", you already know that you have a gap - and you can progress to the next step by asking - "do I really know the gap"?

The age-old wisdom of "Know Thyself" is so apt here - whatever growth we want, all the fulfilment and self-actualisation we are looking for, is about moving as close to segment 1 as possible.

This question- **to our own deepest, most honest mirror, is the starting point to that journey**.

We are not asking you to get into a fault-finding exercise. Instead, we want you to ask yourself this question with a **genuine desire to grow** and it can have a profound impact on you finding your v2.0 and play it full.

Kapil: This happened to me a decade back, when in response to my request for change, my manager asked me to start managing business development for APAC region for the BU I worked in, as I was really bored with my work. His rationale was that because of my high creativity, I will make significant headways in growing business where there were almost none.

I actually thought he was joking about my creativity. I remember saying "Madhu, my creativity is limited to naming my daughter "kapil.k"!!

However, he made me realise, how he was always able to leverage this side of mine and how my client relationships were based on that strength of ideation and creativity.

I discovered an amazing thing about me then - something that I just couldn't have done but for the nudge and guidance from my manager.

This was a turning point in my career as I got access to a deep strength inside that has never left me since.

You too can relate to it. You have had such instances when you discovered your strength in a specific area **once you opened yourself up for the opportunity**. That kind of a spectacular discovery and growth ALWAYS started with a question.

So, what is the question you are asking yourself today?

Shilpa: Two years back, as we were lying on a beach, with a group of friends, admiring the full moon and the way waves danced with an enchanting rhythm under its silver light, I asked a question "How far is this moon from us?"

As Kapil brought out his knowledge of Cosmology to give a factual answer, one of our friends snapped in between, "Leave it, let's not get into facts here, they take away all the beauty".

Really?

Knowing and diving deep into facts, how can they take away that beauty? In fact, as you get closer to the facts, you combine romantism with it, making the feeling more beautiful and real.

In fact, this incident immediately reminded me of a book called "Un-weaving the Rainbow", the world-famous microbiologist Richard Dawkins argued that those who don't want to know how the rainbow is made say that "It will take its beauty away", are missing a significant idea. By knowing how it is created, its beauty will become bigger, because it will no longer be an awe of unknown but an awe of both seeing and knowing its beauty. It will no longer be ignorance but driven by the awareness.

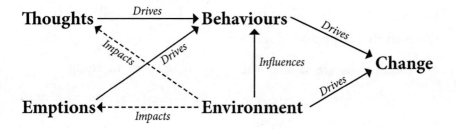

A critical component of understanding ourselves is the "House of Change" model that explains how we mostly focus on the behavioural elements and environment constraints, when we want a change of state or when we want to accomplish a goal.

If instead, we focus on the **thoughts** and **emotions**, it will create a more lasting change as you would able to attack the underlying thought process.

Entire awareness process is derived out of this idea of focusing on thoughts and emotions, then leading to the behaviours we want to inculcate.

Let us further understand the context by considering a viral post on social media sometimes back.

There was a monk, who decided to do meditation at a lake. The monk took a boat to the middle of the lake. As he was in the trance, he heard a loud noise and the next second, his boat shuddered due to the impact of another boat crashing into his. He started getting very angry and opened his eyes to shout at the ignorant fool who crashed into him.

There was no one, only a boat that had lost its anchorage. That shook the monk. He realised that the anger was inside him.

There is nothing in this story that you already do not know. But right now, when all your senses are primed to increase your awareness, consider this story and how you exist **independent of** the stuff that happens around you.

You can **choose** to react the way you like – to anything!

This "Be Aware" step is covered in 3 specific actions you must take to create deep awareness:

A. Understand your Limiting beliefs

B. Understand why you have them by discovering your story and letting it go

C. Develop powerful beliefs

The steps you must take to get this part make the biggest impact in your life are laid out below.

Understand your Limiting Beliefs

"It is not what you say out of your mouth that determines your life; it is what you whisper to yourself that has the most power"

– Robert T Kiyosaki

Shilpa: Most of my childhood, I was a very average child, whose report card never looked very promising. From a middle-class family, I was struggling to keep my head above water in one of the top schools of Dehradun, India.

I was that under-confident back bencher, hiding in the school corridors, not only from the teachers but also from the students.

In year 11, I chose commerce as a subject to pursue. On day 1 of the year, I took my usual place in the class, hiding in the last seat.

As my new class teacher entered, he said something very profound that changed my life.

"No matter at what level you performed until now, whether you were a topper, an average or struggling, this is your opportunity.

Commerce, Accounts, Economics, Macbeth- these subjects are new to each of you in this class of 50. It will be like another opportunity to learn your A, B, Cs and depending upon how committed you are and the amount of efforts you put in, you will go forward in life."

I felt as if someone had thrown a bucket of icy cold water on my face on a winter morning.

I gathered my books, my bag and all my confidence and walked to the front seat. Someone at the back laughed and the entire class started laughing.

I still remember, I was about to go back to the back seat but all of a sudden realised that the sound I was hearing was not that of laughter but of cheering!

I straightened my back and looked up at my teacher, who gave me a knowing look and smiled warmly.

And I never left that seat. The world wanted me to succeed.

That quarter, I got 1st rank in most subjects and in the next, and that continued until I topped the entire Commerce section in school for year 12 board and later went on to hold an All India rank in my Chartered Accountancy Exam.

How did this become possible?

Because:

I recognized the opportunity to start afresh.

I decided to let go of my past failures.

I got the right mentor to coach me.

And I went ALL IN.

Past impacts you significantly more than you think and knowing this can really create a space for growth. The key is to let go and start afresh.

That day can be TODAY!

In the Johari Window in the previous section, the "Blind Spots" is where your limiting beliefs hide.

Let us work on helping you discover what seat you have to give up.

There are 3 type of limiting beliefs that holds us back.

A. *Limiting beliefs about the world*

These beliefs are deep rooted in the long-gone ideas that this is the way the world is and you cannot do anything about it.

An example is "The world is a dangerous, selfish place".

Mostly, this belief is around the rules, written or perceived. The automatic habit cultivated by our environment ensures that we abide by them, without acknowledging that we have a power to change it.

B. *Limiting beliefs about others*

These are how we see other individuals around us.

An example would be "most people are out there to take advantage of us".

These kinds of beliefs can be put to rest by **increasing interaction with other people** and making a genuine effort to connect with them.

C. *Limiting beliefs about ourselves*

These are the most damaging beliefs we hold on to because of our past trauma and experiences.

An example is "I get lucky in life".

In most cases, it was a small incident or interaction long back, where you decided how you ought to be and you got stuck there. These are the hardest beliefs to break.

Let us do a simple exercise to find these:

Complete these sentences – what is the first thing that comes to your mind? Do not give yourselves more than 2-3 seconds to answer.

Limiting beliefs about the world:

The only way to get rich in this world is to _____.

In order to be successful in the world, you have to _____.

Limiting beliefs about others:

Most rich people are _____.

The world is full of _____ people.

Limiting beliefs about ourselves:

I am scared of _____.

I cannot be _____.

Have a look at the above 6 points and pick those **that have a serious negative impact on you!**

These are your limiting beliefs.

These are things that create a challenge in your life as to how you deal with situations and how you find yourself living a life that has many elements out of place.

If it still doesn't give you, do the above exercise again and this time consider negative associations with the sentences.

If you still are not able to identify it, consider what you think is wrong with the world around you. What is wrong with people and where you don't fit in.

The limiting belief you have are primarily related to how you are as compared to the world you see. Things like, "I am not enough", or "I am too old", or "I am too young", or "I need approval from people" etc.

In some cases, these can get so severe that you feel like blurting out to people "You won't understand it. You don't know what I went through." This is mostly in cases when someone has gone through a physical or mental abuse in the past.

In other cases, you may have beliefs that stem from your environment such as "Things have to move slowly in order to be sustainable".

Those could be rationalisations we have about why we don't want to move any faster.

Shilpa: One of my limiting belief was that "It is not possible to be truly yourself in a large group". This created a lot of challenges. It was really illogical and I never remembered when I developed it but it gave me a reason to rationalise my fear of expression in large group settings.

A critical element of the limiting belief is that there is some hidden benefit of holding on to it. If that doesn't make sense, let us take some examples and explore the possible benefits of holding on to that belief:

Limiting Belief	Possible benefit of holding on to it
I am not enough	Sympathy, not trying hard, letting others work, letting yourself go off the hook
I get lucky/unlucky in life	Avoid hard work, avoid responsibility, being lazy while others work, avoid ownership
No one helps another person without ulterior motive	Remain cynical about issues with the world without taking responsibility, others will sympathize
I am too old	Avoid risks, responsibilities, thinking and DOING big things
I am not intelligent	Others will sympathize, letting me be safe in my cocoon, justify the stay in my comfort zone

There is always some benefit of holding on to these beliefs. The benefits often come in the form of avoidance of something that is **perceived** to be either difficult or risky.

Let us consider, what do you need to do to get rid of your past.

Understand your Story

> *"Your mind is a meaning-making machine. Most of the time, without even trying, you 'know' what things mean"*

> **– Unknown**

Our beliefs are based on our experiences. Something would have happened in your life that would have given birth to that feeling and you got trapped in that story forever, with those beliefs pulling you down all the time.

Shilpa: For a long time, I had a limiting belief that I am not a good presenter and I cannot present effectively to an audience.

With my coach, I drilled into my life and found the root of this belief. I found my story- my problem was not with the presentations but with memory retention.

This is what had happened:

When I was 10-year-old, I went on stage with a lot of enthusiasm for a show, but I forgot my dialogue midway and I froze on the spot, standing embarrassed in front of the whole school.

What followed was me running down the stairs red-faced, embarrassed and hearing a series of laughers from the audience.

The story that I carried in my mind from that day affected how I dealt with stage ever after.

I became so scared of forgetting that even while presenting, my mind was always focused on recalling the next part, affecting my delivery.

Once I acknowledged the story behind my limiting belief, I decided to take a look at it factually.

What had happened that day?

Emotions aside, what really happened was that I went on stage, I forgot my lines and the audience laughter.

That's it.

I may have done the same if I was in the audience- no one did it with any ill-feeling towards me, in fact most of them did not even know me nor would they ever know. In other words, my embarrassment was of my own making. Once I got to the facts of that story, it was easy for me to let go of it.

My next challenge was to face my fear in the face- I registered myself for a great 5 days training by Benjamin J Harvey in Sydney and learnt memory retention concepts that created a powerful place for me to start from.

Boom.... my limiting beliefs disappeared and I started my journey as a Presenter, as a Speaker. I would have never walked that path, if I hadn't let go of my story that essentially said, "I can't".

When you let go of your story – you discover a new power inside you!

Let us go through another story that will help you identify your story and then let go of that limiting belief.

We were once in a 3.5 days personal development seminar with 160 other people. The format of the seminar was that people shared their stories and the coach dug deep into it to help them understand the underlying beliefs and challenges.

There was a 72 years old 5 Ft 8 inches tall man always sitting in the back seat – even when people were encouraged to move around during every break.

Let us call him John. John had deep creases on his face – not all of them seemed like that of old age. He looked way too old even for his age.

On the 3rd day, towards the fag end of the course, John raised his hands to share something.

He narrated that when he was 6 year' old, he was at the school and had dysentery and accidentally soiled himself. As he walked back from school, he had many children laughing at him and making comments. That was the most shameful walk of his life.

Over next 66 years, he allowed that incidence to literally impact every aspect of how he dealt with people around him. He would not allow a walk of shame ever and he closed his world to everyone. He became tough for everyone around him, including his own family.

He further shared that it came together during his retirement party in office where a tall, 6 ft 3 inches, strongly built man said how he has always been scared of Mr John.

Narrating this story, John had tears in his eyes when he said "that day after my retirement, I came back home and cried like a baby. I knew I had won my battle of being feared but lost everything else." All those little joys and happiness lived outside the walls of the tough world he had created for himself.

"What I realised now when I got in touch with that 6 year old boy was that I had allowed a 6 year old boy to rule my entire life and ruin it", he continued.

There were probably only a few people in the audience who didn't have tears listening to this.

We all have baggages and they crept on our back when we are very small.

It started with that seemingly simple statement that we perceived to be something else entirely – but it created a small micro tear in that base of life that we are carefully building.

Then as we grow, we are asked to not do certain things or tough situations happen and we have another miro rupture introduced in our concrete base.

Things keep happening and we keep allowing these micro ruptures to get accumulated.

Until one day....

Until one day, something happens in our life – something as simple as the tall, strongly built man or woman seemingly gives a compliment to us, which creates a fissure. And we realise what a wrecker we have been. How we have allowed life to happen to us rather than controlling the flow.

What is your baggage? What is your story?

What have you been carrying on your back all these years?

"I am not good enough" – they must never find out

"I will never be loved" – they must never be allowed to hurt me

"I want my parents to approve of me" – they must be satisfied with what I do

The list would be endless...

What is your story?

What has been that single theme that has governed your entire life?

You may dismiss it saying that it may have served you well because you never knew any better but isn't that starting to becoming a source of constant pain?

Isn't that thorn constantly pricking you in the side?

How good would it be to find it and get rid of it?

Let us find out.

What do people find annoying about you? What can't they ever trust you? What is a recurring pattern in your life that you do NOT like?

Kapil: In my case, it was my overzealous, imposing solutions on everything that others find annoying.

You feel the need to ask some trusted friend – why do they find it annoying?

I was told that – "it is irritating that you seem to believe you have an answer to everything, even when we know for sure you don't. You sometimes throw random statistics to prove your point"

"Proving my point". Interesting.

But WHY?

Because I wanted to fit in. Because I wanted to get approval from them.

I then discovered that getting approval from people was the single biggest driving factor of my entire life.

And I discovered my story that I had shared earlier about the brilliant fan I built!

Ask few of your friends and find out what is that annoying stuff you have?

What more you can do to discover your story?

Each of us have a story. Each of us...you may disagree to start with but make a genuine effort to find it....and you will.

Is it important to find this story?

Yes, if you want to become unstoppable in your life and career – you MUST find it and put it to rest.

Let us warn you – an intellectual understanding of this is **not going to cut it**. You MUST find it and close it – best scenario would be talking to the person who was the direct cause of it.

It is likely to be something that you remember vividly, when you were 6-10 year of age.

Why that age? Because that is the age where your rational faculties are developing but not yet developed. That is also the age when maximum number of synapses in your brain get disconnected – and some connections that should have been severed but didn't, created a meaning out of a meaningless situation.

That memory will be very vivid and clear even today – when you find it. The pain associated with what happened will be still present and your insecurities will come out.

You can also find that story by writing down that one repeated behaviour in your life that you don't understand about yourself, that you want to get rid of. The story is likely hidden there.

If you cannot find that pattern yourself, interview 5 people who know you very well. Include close family members, friends and maybe even a colleague- some one that you spend most time with.

Before interviewing, let the person know that you would not defend anything.

Q1- What can you always depend on me for?

Q2- What can you never depend on me for?

Q3- What does everyone in the world who knows me, knows about me?

Q4- If I must change one thing about me, what do you think it should be?

This will give you a good idea of the common pattern you have followed across your entire life.

Write down the pattern here

_____

_____

_____

There is massive growth hidden behind what you wrote above.

Pick the one that is the MOST painful.

Consider that it is a mask you wear in public and that you almost always know, that this is a mask.

Kapil: For instance, I wore mask of a well-informed guy (in science).

Don't get me wrong, I love science and all the amazing surprising stuff but because I have a positive association of "learning is sharing" and disliked hard work, I found the middle ground of knowing only surface level stuff and then throw it around to get approval or impress people.

It allowed me to fit in very well and become the centre of any discussion.

However, when it was about going into the depth– I avoided getting into that or just threw stats. When it came to actually talking to people and holding attention and arguing in-depth on something, I used to change topics and absolutely hated attention.

When it came to proving something, I referred to stats as if I was the one who wrote the white paper in the reputed journal – clearly leveraging half knowledge to justify my points!

Clearly it is a sign of someone who wants approval more than anything else but doesn't want to quite get there!

Once you get a similar pattern about yourself, think of a time when you were 6-10 year-old, when something happened to you.

Something simple but the underdeveloped brain of that child absorbed it differently and it never quite changed.

Many of these useless connections in the brain (synapses) got strengthened because of the story or the meaning you created?

None of what we do, is an exact science. If your brain is run by a 500 trillion Synapses, it is definitely going to concatenate a reality that is not completely true.

What happens when you find your story!

You will know that it is that story you are suffering with, when you physically feel the punch in your stomach!

What do you do when you get your story?

In simple words - *Get over it*.

But let us get into details –

First, you must write it down- feeling all the pain associated with it and the emotions involved.

Next, imagine going back to that incident and looking at it from the sky. See the big picture- imagine what time of the day it was, summers or winters, day or night – see what happened, what did you do, where were the other characters before that incident, why did they act the way they did.

Now, write down that story again- this time factually, as you saw from the top, without feeling the pain. Remember to keep emotions aside this time and concentrate only on the facts.

Then talk to the person who was most associated with that incident, that story – who you were responding to when the incident happened. Pick up the phone and talk to him, to close the story with that person.

Kapil: I closed my story of "are you crazy" with my dad in Dec 2017, when I visited him in the US. Though I had found my story in May and intellectually closed it in my head, talking to him about it created completely new space in my life.

The conversation was not as hard as you would imagine. I was coming from the place of acceptance and how it was all me, who made up that story.

I would strongly encourage you to close the story. And don't blame them, don't expect understanding or anything. You are not talking about it to be loved, appreciated or anything else. You are talking about it to put your mind at rest forever.

This "talk" shouldn't be about what he/ she did to you. **It has to be about how you wrongly perceived it**. No blame on others – or you will create another story and a reason to continue to play hide and seek with yourself.

And then,

Let it go!!!

It was something that happened. It existed in past and has got NO bearing on your life today.

Stop carrying it because it impacts you massively in ways you don't fully realise. It shows up in your communication with your boss, with your teams and with yourself.

"Pain is inevitable, suffering is a choice."

– An Old Buddhist Saying

The choice is yours and yours alone.

This is your day!

It doesn't matter how you are doing in your life until today-whether you are outstanding, average or struggling. It doesn't matter what your constraints are, it doesn't matter what beliefs you have.

Today is your opportunity to gather your books and go to the first row and sit there. You don't have to figure out what you will do there.

Just get up and make a start!

This very act will change the way you think and act from this day onwards and will redefine your success in life.

Define Powerful, Empowering Beliefs

> *"Hack your past with forgiveness, hack your present with mindfulness, hack your future with 'I am enough'"*
>
> **– Vishen Lakhiani**

Now when you know your limiting beliefs, why they exist and you have been able to let go of your story, it is time to discover your new beliefs and access an already existing powerful force inside you.

Let us dwell upon these limiting beliefs again to continue the context:

For example, if your limiting belief is "I am too busy", the real question will be "why is it so?" Is that an excuse you are giving to yourself because it allows you to **get off the hook** for doing things that you do not consider a priority?

Look around at the most successful people in this world. How do they have all the time in the world to do what they want?

You may want to argue that they are rich, so they have other people working for them and they have all the liberty to focus on what they really want. Do not underestimate the point that these people got there by working hard.

These people were just like us when they started off. They started small, in fact in most cases, they were in a much worse shape than us. But they used their adversity as a fuel to push it forward.

Gary Vaynerchuk, who has a net worth of US$150 million, has all the time in this world to go to garage sales to prove his point that anyone can make money if they want.

And here we are!

With all the luxuries that we own, we hold on to them tightly as if they are our ultimate goal in life.

We wear the cloak of being contented and use it as an excuse to stay average.

We learn to be ok with our mediocre life and stick to it till the day we die.

However, the people who have a millionaire mindset do not give themselves any reason to stay mediocre.

Now is the time to get rid of those beliefs that are chaining you, holding you back and not allowing you to flourish.

And adopt new Empowering Beliefs.

If your limiting belief was "If I don't do it, it will not get done well", your new belief can be "I always optimise my time" – *out goes the busy bee!*

If your limiting belief was "I do not have the confidence", your new belief can be "I create the result I desire" – *out goes confidence from the equation!*

If your limiting belief was "It will go wrong, unless I analyse it well", your new belief can be "I am an action man/woman" – *out goes overthinking or analysis by paralysis!*

Write this new empowering belief for every limiting belief that you identified earlier. The nature of this new belief must be such that the previous one goes out of the window and it actually solves something substantial in your life. In some cases, it is even fine to have 2 new beliefs replace an old one.

Come up with 2-3, crisp, clear, succinct empowering beliefs (more than three is a noise).

Now write them down in big bold writing and stick to your fridge or on a wall where you can see and speak them out daily.

Kapil: My most empowering beliefs now are

    A. I always have a lot to contribute to every person I meet

    B. My authenticity is so visible that everyone trusts me – they can't help it!

Needless to say, A makes me comfortable in any situation – out goes any confidence issues or fitting in issues.

B continuously creates a need in me to be true to my word always and my being.

Your new beliefs are powerful and there is a pleasant surprise in store here. To get there, do the below exercise.

Consider your accomplishments so far in life. No matter what you do, you would have tons of professional and personal accomplishments in your life.

Write at least 5 of them- Your Accomplishments:

- big or small, which make you extremely proud

- where you were surprised by the results that you created in those instances

- which were created by YOU, using your PERSONAL Power and not just as a support.

Shilpa: One of my mentees was going through a rough patch in her career as her company had to let her go. None of it was due to any fault of hers.

Her mind was so clogged with the tensions in her life that she couldn't think of even a single accomplishment to start with. As we continued to probe, she started talking about some of the things she did – a little sheepishly at first and then strongly. She recalled an instance where she had saved her company hundreds of thousands of dollars with her initiatives, and soon she was discovering amazing accomplishments one after the other!

You too have amazing accomplishments in your life and your career and maybe those low times, diminished the importance of them.

Maybe it is because you now are in a more senior role or you have higher standards and you forgot how you were once given the youngest manager award or how with only 2 years of experience, you were promoted as a team lead, or you solved that huge problem on site single handedly?

If your mind is clogged and you are not able to find it – start writing it down and it will come back floating.

Write down 3 accomplishments in your life that you are extremely proud of.

In front of each accomplishment, write down your 3 new beliefs in the columns 2 to 5.

See example below:

Accomplishments	Empowering Beliefs		
	I am confident	I take initiatives	Everyone Trusts me
I saved the company 100,000$ with my initiative in XYZ	X	X	
I got a new contract signed up by the client based on my current performance	X		X

You will discover that you **always had those empowering beliefs!**

You have already accomplished great heights, based on those beliefs. You are not doing anything new. You don't need to test these new beliefs. You have already been exhibiting these, as part of your best accomplishments.

Embrace them fully as your Beliefs. They are yours!

STEP 2 – CREATE YOUR FUTURE

"I want the world to be better because I was here."

- Will Smith

Now it is time to create the future of your choice.

People think that vision, mission, goals are only for the rich and successful people. The irony is that these people are successful by the very fact that they have a purpose, vision, mission and goals.

When you identify a purpose in life, you are 4-5 times more likely to succeed. The reason is simple, your eyes are set towards the future and the obstacles and constraints in front, become simple roadblocks to be removed and not something to fret over.

People without a purpose in such cases will either jump the ship, or change their targets or just give up and go back to their earlier ways.

What we hear in media further makes it complicated.

We hear more about failures than successes. Those who become successful, their stories don't come out till they are super successful – and by that time, those stories have become way too big for most people to relate to.

Everyone who has been spectacularly successful and out of average game has a mission, a purpose, that they are serving. This is true for people from all walks of life, irrespective of eastern or western philosophies.

For those, who believe that they are not goal people but journey people, they need to understand that the two are not mutually exclusive but part of the same coin.

One without the other is utterly useless and it is akin to floating in the water. Would you rather be floating in water or swimming in its wake and deciding when and where to go?

"Life is meant to be lived at its peak and not at the bottom! Contrary to what we have learnt, there is happiness, contentment, love, joy and connection at the peak as well."

– Kapil K

Your goals are your road to that peak.

The joy is not just in the achievement of the goals, but in becoming the person you have the potential to become. The happiness that you are bound to feel is in the progress along that path that is forward moving and not zigzagging violently!

Your goal should be a combination of the 3Ps- **Purpose, Passion and Prosperity.**

If you are living someone else's purpose, generating wealth (prosperity) but are not passionate about it, it is not the best for you.

Also, if you are living your purpose and passion but you are not generating wealth along with it, how far will you go?

Average people play ball by ball, reacting to events or circumstances in life. However, the real fun begins when you are in the driver's seat, and know fully well what destination you have fed in your GPS. And as you start driving towards it, you keep enjoying the breeze from the open windows.

A lot of people start with "I do not know what my goal is" and it is ok. Everything has to start somewhere.

Let us go through the step by step process. You don't have to get it right today. You have to just get started and refine as you go along. Having a partner, a coach or a mentor, someone who can use his or her experience of working with others, will definitely speed it up significantly.

Let us first define what these words mean – so that we can speak the same language.

Purpose deals with why do you exist? This is not something driven by your circumstances, your personality or others. It is why do YOU think you exist.

Kapil: I exist to share and enable others to play it full in their lives. Simple, personal and direct.

Shilpa: As an enemy of the average game, exist to pull people from an average game to create an outstanding life of their choice.

Your purpose is visible to almost anyone who deals with you.

They may not trust that it is who you are depending on their own personality but it is visible to them and within a matter of time they agree.

Vision: What future do you envisage – for the world and the environment around you.

For instance, our vision is to enable 1 million people to make conscious choices to become their best version and live their version 2.0.

Vision is what keeps you turning the wheel in the right direction.

Mission: Your mission becomes a driver for you and defines how you would reach your vision. It is that unique way, that is aligned with your style, values, your core, which will help you get to that vision.

For instance, our mission is to create a personalised, high energy, high impact coaching organisation that helps people get past their average game and play it full across the Triangle of Life.

Identity: Who do you NEED to become to make your vision a reality?

For instance, we constantly talk about who do we need to become to be the person, who will impact 1 million people. As our proximity changes, as we learn more, as we grow, we keep moving forward in that direction.

You don't have to be 100% clear about it during the start of this journey.

Goals: This are specifics milestones that you must achieve in a timely way to keep moving towards your vision.

The Values and Standards will be covered in next section but it is apt to talk about it here.

Values: Values are the compass that tell you that you are on the right path.

It is easy to get lost. We have all known people who started out right but somewhere down the line, they got diverted from their path and ended up in a very bad place.

Values ensure that it doesn't happen.

Standards:

Standards are the personal norms you set for yourself. "This is the bare minimum", you say. You never go below your standard, whether someone is watching or not.

Purpose, Vision, Mission & Identity

"Great Minds have Purpose; others have wishes"

– Washington Irving

Define Your Purpose

You have worked on your story that created the negative association and found a pattern that had kept you in chains.

Sure enough, there are also strong positive beliefs, you must have for being where you are today. In the previous section, you saw that you were already working with several set of positive beliefs.

Pick up the strongest empowering belief, the one that seems to be woven throughout your life.

If you can find that one single positive pattern throughout your life, what is it?

There is a strong positive association in your brain about this already and you would do well to tap into that uniqueness that already exists. It is time to find that positive story from your life, which still creates warmth and positive feelings.

Find that pattern, that story and positive association.

Kapil: When I did this exercise years back, I found one story of when I was a child. I don't recall why but my father's elder brother said to him about me, "this boy has so much love to give to everyone".

The way this came out in my life was to always think, how something can become better. I recall, getting into a shop and having this insane drive to suggest to owner about how they can move things around to sell it better. The Play It Full was visible even when I was a child.

I didn't always play to my full potential in past and wasted too many precious years engineering smallness in my life – but this feeling now has become this insatiable hunger for people to take the steps to find themselves and start living their version 2.0.

It is almost like, when I am not doing this, I feel frustrated.

In the process of setting up my coaching business, those have always been the low points for me – when I see prospects staying in denial and struggling.

Make your "Purpose" go through the same test and define it.

And do not worry about getting it right. Get started, date the purpose like you date someone you met for the first time and see how it evolves. It is so personal to you that you can change it when you want.

It is not defined to make others feel great, it is the core of WHO YOU ARE.

Define Your Vision

If you have a magic wand and have the power to change the world in any shape or form, how would you like it to be? Consider if money was not a constraint and you had unlimited resources, what would you do?

_____

_____

_____

For that, you would like to look back at your life and see the positive stories, associations and patterns that have always existed and leverage them to see what would make you feel the goose bumps.

Add measurable outcomes on it – in terms of lives impacted – as specific as you can. You must also have a destination – where will this take you or the kind of people you are impacting?

Don't worry about getting it perfect or about other people liking it. Start and you will get there. In the later section, where we discuss values, we have a technique to help you refine your vision.

"If you know where you are going, you have better chances of arriving there."

– Shilpa K

Define Your Mission

What specifics path do you need to walk on to get there? What is your vehicle to go to that vision?

For us, it is a coaching organisation and it is about that fight against the average game.

What is your vehicle?

Consider if you were doing it for someone else, what ways could you think that they can reach that vision?

Make a list of 5 things that come to your mind. Then pick the one that feels right.

This may not be entirely correct. You again have to date it a bit by leveraging others or by talking to your coach.

You may get lucky if you do it in isolation. However you are significantly more like to succeed if you get an outside eye to help you look beyond your own limitations, to see what is possible.

This one takes time – so don't worry if it is not clear right at this moment. Maybe when you read this book twice or thrice, you will get it.

Define Your Identity

In a talk during National Achiever's Congress, Sydney in 2019, Elena Cardone made a very apt statement. She said that she was constantly pushing Grant Cardone to reach a level to manage $10B from the $1.2B funds they currently manage through Cardone Capital.

Maybe by the time you read this, they would have gone way beyond that!

> *"It is not the number that matters, it is who we become in that pursuit that matters more"*
>
> **– Elena Cardone**

Who would you have to become in the process of getting that Vision realised?

That is your identity.

Shilpa: I see myself as an Influencer, Leader, Author and a Speaker. That is who I have to become to realise my vision. That is what drives my mission, my goals and what I do every day.

Your identity can be a world leader or a community influencer or an impactful speaker or a wealth generator or a change agent who is at a battle with the status quo. It is almost like, when you say that others feel compelled to ask, "tell me more".

Your identity may change with time and as you learn more. Bringing grandeur to this is a good idea usually but being too general such as "a happy person" is too cliché – "A Happiness Generator" is rather good on the other hand, since it has to be about how your identity is aligned with the outcome you generate.

Define your Identity and your life will never be same!

Define it and share on **"playitfull"** Facebook page – let your community work for you and give you feedback!

Defining Your Goals

"Whatever you hold in your mind on a consistent basis is exactly what you will experience in your life."

– Tony Robbins

During 2018 UPW (Unleash the Power Within) Program with Tony Robbins, he shared an amazing story. When he started coaching people at 17 years of age, he made $38K in the first year. He did have a great list of clients and was working with millionaires at such an early age.

One day, a client called him to meet him at his place that the client intended to rent out. When Tony reached there, he found that this was actually a castle, with all the porches and the roof style, etc. During the conversation, the client asked him why doesn't he take it on rent at $6600 per month?

Tony at the time was staying in a $450 per month room, which was a small 4X4 room, that included his office, his table and his hammock to sleep on – as he didn't have enough place to put a bed there.

Tony decided to take the castle for rent. This was illogical, unreasonable and completely against his rather lower-middle-class upbringing. But he decided to back himself up.

Next year, Tony made $1M.

Fast changes are possible only if you have a target, a goal to look at and get energised and obviously, if you back yourself up. Goals allow us that dream, that hunger and help us identify ways, in which we can break our existing patterns!

It is probably true that you hate the idea of a goal because, in the corporate world, the goals were set up mostly by others. Added to that is a painful association that not meeting goals, results in financial pains, rebukes or some other negative outcome.

Majority of people do not have a concrete goal other than "being happy", which is so subjective. Pursuing your dream is about having specificity in defining those dreams.

> *"Goals are like magnets. They'll attract the things that make them come true."*
>
> **– Tony Robbins**

Consider the journey of Bhaskar Maddala, the CEO of Alpha IT Australia. He grew to executive levels in large IT service companies in a very short time.

He recalls that from the beginning, he was very target oriented and mentioned that throughout his career, he always knew what he wanted and it always so happened that he got that eventually. He had no doubts whatsoever about specificity of his goals and ensured they were really written down in his diary for him to see every day.

Setting goals ensures that you have a direction, before you start playing a powerful game in life.

The goals are like the lamp posts to your destination, your vision and give you a measurable indication of how well you are going.

Let us make the goals simple and easy to do by breaking it down and focus on one level at a time.

Level 1: **Your Identity – who would you be? Your BE Goal**

This is something you want to implement – not just leave on paper. This is what you want to be known for or leave a legacy for. It is almost like "to be that person who will do XYZ"

Imagine you are in a helicopter and you look at that **future you** from the top. What would you see yourself as? If you were to visualise that future, what will you see in your surroundings? What impact would you be making?

There may be a temptation in having 10 such goals but remember, less is more in this case.

Define one single BE goal.

Write down

To be _____

So that I can build _____

Once you have done that, split your BE goal across the 3 areas of the Triangle of Life and answer the following questions:

What does this goal mean for my Achievements and the Impact I would like to create?

_____

What does this goal mean for my Health? How do I have to show up every day for this BE Goal?

_____

What does this goal mean for my Relationships? How do I have to be with myself, with people around me and the communities at large?

_____

Adjust your BE goal based on the above musings. Being able to clearly define what it means for each segment indicates that you have got something powerful brewing in your head!

Level 2: Achieve Goals – What are the 3 things you have to achieve in order to get to that BE Goal?

These are the milestones in your beautiful journey of life.

Achieve goals are time bound and specific. They are not a TO Do List. These are things you want to achieve, that are in alignment with your BE goal.

For instance, becoming a CEO of an organisation may give you the influence that is a base for you to stand on and launch another phase of your career.

Level 3: Do Goals – What do you have to actually DO to achieve each Achieve Goal?

Each of these achieve goals can now be broken into steps. For instance, if the achieve goal is to become an author, a "do goal" could be about starting a blog or writing a book.

Though, these shouldn't be operational kind of things, such as "write a blog per month", while it is measurable, it is not time bound. Rather, you should say, "write a blog by the first of every month".

There may be a temptation to do a "To-Do List" that is extremely detailed but it is best to avoid it otherwise, all that you would be doing is writing and then get overwhelmed.

We recommend writing up to 3 DO Goals for each achieve goals and set the timelines within next 3-6 months – no further.

And also remember that it can change as things unfold in the future. Setting a date would allow you to be on top of your goal and validate the reason for changes, if any.

A lot of people also add the Do Goals in their calendars – so that they are aware of these milestones as they approach it. Some people we coach put it up at a visible place in their house.

We are big fan of "visible" sheets at home – that way you can see it anytime.

Also lock them in your calendar.

If there is any vagueness in your mind, don't be concerned. All you have to do is to start working consistently towards those goals, as the path becomes clearer along the way and the journey becomes enjoyable.

Kapil: One of my mentees has a vision of transforming rural landscape in India to become self-sustainable. For that, one of the achieve goal he has is around building a large enterprise creating relevant products for leveraging it in next 5 years (can't share any more specifics)

Vision board

It is also time to get your Vision Board set up.

Get an A3 size paper and put it up on a visible place at your home. Keep it away from prying eyes so that it is very personal without social concerns.

On the top Centre – write your **Purpose**

Below that your **Vision**, then **Mission**.

Declare your **Identity**

Below that write down your empowering **beliefs** (that you found in section 7.1.3)

Below that leave space for your Values, Your Strengths and Your Standards and fill later once you have gone through next section.

Stick 6 A4 papers below it and write down your Do Goals- one on each paper and also obstacles that you need to overcome for that goal. Use coloured circles to make it visually simple for you to follow.

By now, you would be feeling very powerful, confident and clear. If not, we suggest stop reading this and actually DO the exercises above before you continue.

This process is not useful unless you implement it. In fact, NOTHING is useful unless you DO something with it!

STEP 3 – MASTER YOUR SELF

"It is not that we have so little time but that we lose so much. ... The life we receive is not short but we make it so; we are not ill provided but use what we have wastefully."

- Lucius Annaeus Seneca, (4 BC-65 AD)

Though we really hope there is no one asking now, what mastering your 'self' has got to do with being unstoppable in your career!

One last response to that – You are one whole person – if you want small changes, you improve things as you notice them. If you want massive changes, discover yourself and be **powerful in perpetuity!**

Self-mastery is about knowing your strengths, your values, your standards and strong set of beliefs, your unique abilities and your own pockets of brilliance. It is about taking control of your Triangle of Life – achievements, health and relationships, setting standards and creating that powerful you.

Knowing who you are and working to strengthen your core, ensures that you are oozing with energy and confidence, while presenting yourself and dealing with the outside world.

Mastering Your Technical Skills

"Know your core competencies and focus on being great at them"

– Mark Cuban

These are the skills that you have always worked so hard for. This is also related to your college degrees, the certifications you worked for, the trainings you attended. These skills are the demand of the market today and allow you to be employable.

It is not without irony that the skills that you have worked all your life for, invested all your money on, make up only a small part of your personal power. Most of these skills are tactical.

It is almost similar to the Triangle of Life, where most people spend time collecting the low hanging fruit of "Achievement segment".

Similarly, a lot of people consider their growth to be a factor of their college education, certification and courses to keep up with the changing technology.

Don't get us wrong. They are necessary- but we have to put them in perspective. The technical skills are one part of your journey towards self-mastery.

You already know what are the core skillset that you need. Let us talk about how much you need it and what kind of time and money should you spend on it.

Your Core Skills are about the following:

Skills	What does each of them mean?
Technical skills	Your core area – finance, Technology, BA, PM, HR – your growth here is determined primarily by your experience, your certifications and recognitions **This skill gets your noticed by others.**

Work Relationships	This is about how you work with people, your teamwork, your client relationships. Most of these are people who you are working with to deliver the client deliverables. This is more important than Technical Skills as **this is what gets you connects and support** towards your ambition.
Leadership & People Management	How good you are as an influencer in your environment. This is irrespective of your role. If you have people reporating to you, how good you are? Are you a servant leader? This is what you have to master in order **to become unstoppable** in your career.
Stakeholder Management	How well you manage your stakeholders, the decision makers in your organisation? These are the **people who will vouch for you** when the promotion time comes, or when something goes wrong and you need support.
Commercial Acumen	Whether you are beginner or a seasoned person – you need some idea of how money is flowing in your organisation. You have to understand how money moves – or you wouldn't grow in your career beyond a point.
Communication (Presence, Expression, Presentation)	Are you a reactive communicator or do you create possibilities? How do you relate to your listener, how do you express yourself? How do people relate to your presence and talk? This is about your charisma, your presence and influence.

Time Management & Structure	It is true for all levels. Even at the starting rug of the organisation, where everyone expects you to everything, you can use power of leverage and delegate. How are you doing in the Important, Urgent cycle? This is **required to grow** – if you can't, chances are, you will not be promoted!
Thought Leadership (Creative Thinking, Idea & Innovation)	Are you adding massive value? Are you always trying to find out how you can do things better? How do you disrupt your environment positively? How you are perceived in your network?
Above and Beyond	How are you constantly stretching yourself beyond your own expectations of what you do at work?

Now when you understand these, fill up this table with appropriate information

Skills	Current Score	Target Score	Action Plan (consider Certifications, education, mentoring etc) – along with how much impact it makes
Technical skills			
Work Relationships			
Leadership & People Management			
Stakeholder Management			
Commercial Acumen			
Communication (Presence, Expression, Presentation)			
Time Management & Structure			

Thought Leadership (Creative Thinking, Idea & Innovation)			
Above and Beyond			

The last column is the key. Write down specifics, time bound actions and very importantly, the impact of this on the target score.

For instance, you may say that for Technical skills, I should get a Cyber Security Certification and it will 80% relevant to my target score.

The structure is designed to bring out elements that you have not considered before. Working with your coach, you can find things here that were previously not even possible.

For example, one of our mentees, wrote a white paper (his very first white paper) that went on to win global recognition in his organisation of 300,000 people. All he had to do was to remove the noise and focus on what matters.

Keeping yourself updated in your core work area is important in both short and long term. In short term, it creates an opportunity for advancement. In the long term, it creates an opportunity to engage with people, who are at an advanced level and learn from them, leverage them to fuel your growth.

You don't know what you are capable of, till you take time to analyse (put it on paper), evaluate and take actions!

Another critical elements that you need to consider is that just by focusing on your core skill, you would find that your limits reach very fast. Eventually, your growth depends on ensuring that even the core keep changing.

At the core, each business is about creating value for the target customers. It is in that process, businesses make money.

Since everything has to centre around that, your specific job too has to be aligned with that. Your skill upgrading plan therefore has to necessarily consider how you can shift your work to align it with the outcome of creating an outstanding customer experience.

It may look like a big talk and applicable to only senior executives but it is extremely critical to get this right.

Whether you are starting your career or changing it and irrespective of your level, if you can find out how your role is aligned with the need of the end customer, relate it in the form of business problems/solutions and start articulating that in your conversations at work, you will find that it will become very easy to navigate that path.

In our 1-on-1 coaching, this is one of the core premises of growth and often produces spectacular results in a short time.

Identifying Your Values

"Happiness is that state of consciousness, which proceeds from the achievement of one's Values"

– Ayn Rand

Getting our Values articulated is critical as these are really the core of how we operate and act in our life. Value are our moral compass of right and wrong.

Write down your top 5 Values – in life (not in work place – because that would be very restrictive).

Consider how these Values are. Are they behaviours that we like in others or are they values that are borrowed from others based on your social, religious or cultural background? If you were to take these to extremes, consider how will you operate? Will you continue to uphold them?

One of the best process for Value identification, we have seen was created by Authentic Education Pty Ltd (reproduced below with their permission).

The **Value TRACK™** process is defined below (with an example):

	Write here, 3 things	Which of these 3 inspire you most?	What feeling you get from this one? (list 3)
T – What do you love to TALK about	Growth Achievements Unusual Stuff	Growth (This gives me a kick)	Possibilities Forward Movement Contribution
R - What do you love to RESEARCH?	Facts Process Learning	Facts (oh! That is how it happened??)	Credibility Forward Movement Authenticity
A – What skills do you love to ACT upon?	Talking to people Advising Solving	Solving (Yup, I made a difference!)	Energy, Passion! Forward Movement Contribution
C – What do you love to CONTEMPLATE?	How to maximise? What more? Am I doing it right?	How to Maximise (This allows me to share)	Contribution Forward Movement Energy, Passion!
K – What do you KNOW a lot about?	People How things work New Ideas	New Ideas (This gives me a kick)	Forward Movement Authenticity (what I know, I talk about)

Kapil: If you can see, in above example, the words that come out are – Forward Movement, Passion, Contribution, Authenticity.

There! These are my Values!

Let us see how our Values impact our lives, both positively and negatively.

Yes, you read it right – our Values can impact us negatively if they come in conflict with what we see around us. Developing awareness will allow you to handle those situations well.

Since your Values are the moral compass in the journey towards your Vision, these have to be deeply aligned with the Vision. Below is a technique that can be used to test how your Values are aligned with your Vision.

What do you see in your environment at work that annoys you? List them (4-5 things)

_____

_____

What do you see in your environment at home that annoys you? List them (4-5 things)

_____

_____

What do you see in your environment or with friends that annoys you? List them. Consider the commute, coffee shops, shopping, watching movies, just plain walking and seeing things around you.

_____

_____

1. Refine these all across the above 3 questions – cut out the duplicates and create one final list of your annoyances.

2. Next, write down a short description of **why each of the above annoys you.**

When you write down the "Why", you will see that the reason you get annoyed is because of a Value conflict.

Let us now find out what is there in your Value set that makes you label those things as annoying?

Consider the Values that you identified through the above Value TRACK™ model and put them in columns in the table.

Now write down the things that annoy you in the rows.

Create a relationship between the annoyance and Values (up to 5 Values) (putting an X, where you feel a **value conflict** with you and therefore your behaviour/annoyance).

Kapil: Here is an example of some of my annoyances and my Values.

| I get annoyed by | These values get conflicted by the behaviour | | | |
	Authenticity	Passion	Forward Movement	Contribution
When people try to show off without having any depth				X (I am unable to contribute)
People who boss around			X (I stop moving forward)	X (I am unable to contribute)
People talking about things they have no impact on (for instance lounge room talks on politics/religion etc.)			X (I stop moving forward)	X (I am unable to contribute)
Angry people			X (I stop moving forward)	X (I am unable to contribute)
Negative people – who are just finding out what is wrong with the world				X (I am unable to contribute)

Once you are done – have a look and go through the Values that has most Xs below it in the column.

> *Kapil:* For me, this was a shocker! As, it was "Contribution" that created most annoyance for me. Any conflict with that value was unbearable for me.

This specific value, that is High Impact Value is your biggest Value. Something you hold dearest and something that drive you.

This is also where your vision lies.

Have a look back at your Vision. See how aligned it is – if it is aligned, pat yourself in the back. If it is not – this is not congruent and it is likely that the Vision is misunderstood. It is time for you to go back to the drawing board and refine your Vision.

It is easier to identify the Values and unfortunately it is also easy to come up with a Vision that inspires and feels good but doesn't actually feel strong in your heart.

The above exercise is designed to create significant clarity about your Vision.

> *Kapil:* in my case, everyone I meet with, immediately sees my Authenticity and my Passion. This is most visible to others – but the driver for my life is Contribution!

Don't skip this exercise.

The largest benefit of this book is to take notes and do these practical exercises. Else your knowledge will remain half as you are not mastering the execution.

You can put the book down – but do this exercise – it will give you more clarity than any other training has ever done for you.

Action: Write these Values on your Vision Board that you defined in the previous section.

Raise Your Standards

"If you don't set a baseline standard for what you'll accept in life, you'll find it's easy to slip into behaviours and attitudes or a quality of life that's far below what you deserve."

– Tony Robbins

Standards are the norms, you set for yourself. "This is the bare minimum", you say. You never go below your standard, whether someone is watching or not. These are very personal.

Michael Jordan used to say, I am often the first guy on the court and the last guy to leave the gym!

If Values are your compass, your **Standards are the yardstick**, by which you measure yourself.

Consider the story of John Pittard. John left a very senior executive role in a large Australian company – despite being very successful and despite having possibilities of further growth, because of the high standards he had sat for himself.

That turned out to be a turning point in his career.

Discovering your standards is not a hard process.

All you need to do is to again write down your 5 accomplishments.

_____

_____

_____

_____

_____

You must have faced a lot of obstacles during these. There was a reason why you didn't back down. You kept going. What were those reasons? Write down below

_____

_____

The standards you live by are hidden in these reasons.

These are the norms that you have set for yourself, below which you will never go. No matter what happens, they are your "Must to dos'. These are the ones you will not compromise in any situation.

These are your Standards.

> *Shilpa:* Eating healthy is my standard. No matter where I am, even when no one is watching, I live up to that bar that I have set for myself, all the time.

Other thing to look at is: what will advance your growth significantly? What are the behaviours that you must depict that would mean that you no longer do less than what you are capable of?

Define these standards as 2-3 sentences.

_____

_____

Action: Write these Standards on your Vision Board that you defined in the previous section.

Discover Your Strengths

"You will excel only by maximising your strengths, never by fixing your weaknesses"

– Marcus Buckingham

Each one of us have a significant need to do amazingly well in life and keep on growing more and more as individuals.

We all know that if we operate from our strengths, we can achieve our results. However, our environmental challenges do not always allow us to hone these and operate from these.

Consider your social environment – it is filled with trivialities. The discussion over the weekends, the booze sessions with friends, the transactional discussions about others' – many of these are important but trivial matters. We all have to get into these at times.

In this environment, we gravitate to what we do well and what comes easily.

In your work environment however, there are stricter ways to operate, specific behaviours to align with and a way to be. Here, the natural tendency is to focus on things you can improve and change.

It is often difficult to work from your strengths as there are too many people reminding you what is wrong with you and how you can do it better!

We all have been part of the discussion with our managers, where they point out the deficiencies in you, often to the lines of "if you could only fix that one thing, you will be awesome".

In such an environment, it is not a surprise to find that 87% people have felt like an imposter at work place. No matter what they do and how much they grow, there is ALWAYS some inadequacy to deal with.

Instead, if people focus on what they are great at and then bring only that to work place and if people were to learn to leverage it to compensate for their apparent weakness, imagine the impact it will have. Imagine how awesome you will be if you operate from your strengths.

You are already good at something, why not tap into that to take your life to next level?

But what about the weaknesses, you may ask?

As children, most of us grew up with the words: *Do not do this, do not do that, don't go there, don't come here....*

These "DO NOTS" became a way of life and filled our life with a lot of Nos. And then suddenly, we grew older and independent and we were expected to DO things, make decisions, take significant actions. Almost nothing, we do in the early stages of life, prepared us for this life of never-ending choices to make!

It gets complicated further by the corporate appraisal system where the whole emphasis is typically on what we lack and what is wrong with us.

As if, we improve on those 5, 10 or 15 things, we will get promoted the next day.

It is like if you lose all the fat in the body, you will automatically get muscles. Doesn't really happen!

"Forget your weaknesses. They don't matter!"

– Kapil K

Imagine the same efforts that you spend in improving your weaknesses, if you could spend the same amount of effort in sharpening your strengths, the results will be huge!

Your strengths are your silver axe to cut through the random noise in the world- know it, live it, breathe it.

You can certainly improve your weaknesses as much as you want, however you are unlikely to make them as good as what you are already strong at. And these are not things like maths or physics – those are skills. These are things that are part of your character, things such as relating to people, or thinking strategically with options or being analytical.

Your weaknesses therefore are something that you need to find a way to manage. Don't be a lone wolf. Take help!

Let us do an exercise to discover your strengths,

Find 6 adjectives that describe you.

Don't let them be "job specific" or in a corporate lingo. Find your strengths as who you are.

Few examples are "trustworthy", "strategic", "analytical", "adaptable", "action oriented", "independent" etc.

Once you have defined the 6 adjectives, assess them to see if **that is how you have always operated.** Is that how you achieved majority of your success? Consider the accomplishment that you wrote in the previous section and see if these are congruent with the results.

If these are congruent, you can proudly wear those strengths on your sleeve!

You can also leverage online tools for this. The best tools, we have come across is Gallup Strength Finder. There is a $19.99 assessment that immediately gives you a very detailed account of your top 5 strengths. This has been taken by over 21 Million people worldwide. This is something that each of our client use to discover their strengths. The two reports they get at the end of the assessment from Gallup really help them understand their strengths in depth.

Though, just barely getting those 2 reports would not serve you best other than give you something to talk about.

We work with our clients post the online assessment to help them apply it in their life.

While there is a lot that is covered, the most important element is recognising that there are elements of the report that you are not currently implementing in your life. Hidden amongst those sentences is where the largest growth for you lies.

When we work with our clients, this is one of the biggest breakthroughs they get in terms of leveraging their strengths.

Identify your strengths, put them to work – your life will never be same!

Damn Those Obstacles!

"Do not let making a living prevent you from making a life"

– John Wooden

While limiting beliefs are our internal belief systems that impact

the way we do things, obstacles are the external parameters that exist and are perceived to be limiting us in some way or the other.

If you ask people, what are their obstacles, chances are, those will be related to their worries and concerns – bad boss, no opportunity to grow in their company, unsupportive family, not enough money, etc.

We all are aware of our problems, but the only way to solve them is worrying about it enough to feel a massive desire to actually **take actions**.

We all face different types of obstacles.

These are those obstacles that are **surface level**, rather shallow and **primarily related to our convenience**. You can find these immediately and even correct them in the short term. These obstacles are easy to break as they are usually very behavioural.

Typically, people don't worry about because they get some kind of a payback/ benefit from these. In other words, not removing these from your life is either just inconvenient in terms of effort involved or these come up only a few times for you to take notice and you have ways to get around these.

Then there are those obstacles, that are deeper than that. These are related to how we interact with our environment on a day to day basis. These are also about how we believe is "the way to exist in the world". These have been formed due to our upbringing, our experiences in past, especially painful ones, and how we gather new experiences every day.

Let us identify what are the real obstacles and segregate those from the artificial ones.

Consider the 5 top results that you want for yourself. Prioritise these and add 3 columns in front of it.

Column 1- Financial obstacles – like paying bills.

Column 2- Social obstacles – such as invisibility, family pressure etc

Column 3- Internal issues – such as lack of confidence, communication skills etc

Write obstacles in each column in front of each desired result.

For instance, let us take something simple. Let us assume that a result that you desire is "Overseas holiday for a month".

If you start talking about it, you may end up with a lot of perceived obstacles but most of these would be in the periphery.

The real obstacles are much simpler and more direct and writing these down allows you to think through and narrow it down to the really critical ones.

It will look something like this

Desired Results	Financial Obstacles	Social Obstacles	Internal issues
Overseas holiday for 1 month	1- Not enough money in saving account	2- Can't convince my partner 3- My boss won't give me a leave	4- Too much time to plan

Once you write these down – you will see that no 2 and no 4 are actually simple and you can remove those. You also see that no 3 is something you can remove by talking to your boss and finding out what his/her concern is likely to be.

You can then see that the only real thing you have to worry about is no 1.

This makes the desired results suddenly more real. And the overwhelming feeling you had about it disappears simply because of the lower number of obstacles!

This method reduces the potential sources of concerns and helps you find out real obstacles that you can then DO something about.

For example, with your desired result of "overseas holiday", since it is now only about 1 obstacle, you would be more driven to find a resolution without getting overwhelmed.

Now, let us write down what you can do to get over the obstacle

1- find out how much would it cost – split in categories –
- Flight ticket
- Taxi/Cabs
- Stay
- Food
- Entertainment
- Shopping

2- Where can you get the money from.

Continuing with this example – now you can find out how you can minimise expenses. Your diary may look something like this:

1- find out how much would it cost – split in categories –
- Flight ticket – What is cheapest ticket airline? What route can I take – let me search some website for inspiration
- Taxi/Cabs – can I go by train some places? Can I pre-purchase tickets?
- Stay – can I do Airbnb? Will take care of food as well!
- Food
- Entertainment – what is a must do? Can I pre-purchase? Groupon? Deals, Coupons?
- Shopping – plan to minimise, talk to partner

2- Where can you get the money from –
borrow? Sell something? Loan (hope not!), work overtime, temporary job for partner or for weekends? Another hustle? Save money by cutting some expenses?

And so, and so forth.

You can probably see the power of writing things by now.

The issues and obstacles you have, can be removed by following the simple techniques above.

While we took a very simple example, this is just to show you that you can implement it in much any case, including wanting a well desired promotion!

As you can probably see, understanding and implementing these measures will lead to breakthroughs in understanding yourself and mastering your core.

STEP 4 – MASTER YOUR BRAND

"Perception is the co-pilot to reality"

– Carla Harris

Kapil: Back in 2000, I worked for a small start-up of 13 people that barely survived the dot.com burst due to ingenious actions of the CEO and the CIO. As a part of that initiatives, I was chosen to go to Italy for 3 months to execute the project that was a do or die.

It was one of my most challenging assignments ever. I discovered that many Italians typically go on leaves in the month of August. The project manager left for his holidays and as a development lead, I was left holding the fort.

I did a cracking job and when my CIO visited me in Milano, his words were "This is what I know you were capable of", probably the best compliment I ever received.

I came back to the office in Delhi. A part of me expected balloons and dancers and celebration of this massive accomplishment I had.

Nothing happened.

Actually NOTHING. Balloons would have been nice. Some drums would have been nicer! Nothing happened!

Few weeks later, my then boss said that he didn't do anything because he was concerned about how celebrating one individual will make others feel bad.

This was unbelievable! He won't reward someone because others will feel bad!

That became the inflection point for me and I left them when I got the chance to!

I blamed my boss! In reality, I didn't have it inside me to take the control of my life then. I wanted my work to talk about it.

I wanted others to talk about me without having any leverage over them.

Remember Tod's story in the beginning of this book. He didn't manage his brand, how people perceived him. His environment was toxic but it was his mistake that he allowed others to have that kind of a control.

Your life is already awesome, your accomplishments as you have already seen are beyond normal and probably extraordinary. No one else even remembers it but you. No one else is going to talk about it but you.

Creating Your Personal Brand

"For your growth, it doesn't matter who you know but who knows you"

– Gary Vaynerchuk

Since you are reading this book, chances are that either you know us well or have been following us on social media. A very short % would have seen this book in a bookstore and liked the title enough to like it.

It is most likely that you got it because of our brand, our visibility and what you know about us. We obviously believe completely in what we have to offer to the world but no one will buy from us unless they know us, in some shape or form.

This is true in business, in work, and in personal life!

What people know about you and how consistently they hear about you with a cohesive and authentic story, builds your personal brand.

Still, few people consider the fact that building a personal brand is a **deliberate effort**, it must by definition be somewhat "made up".

Carefully think about it. Yes, it is deliberate, but in the world today, it is quite stupid to pretend to be something you are not, as sooner than later, you will be caught. You will end up saying something contradictory at some time or the other and depending on how many people make it their business to know you, you will have to deal with a challenge that you would rather not like.

If you do not manage your brand actively, someone else will. One way or the other, you will end up with a brand image that you may actually dislike heavily.

Besides, why would you want to come across as someone you are not?

To understand the brand that you carry in this world, let's do a simple test.

Write down what do you think of your brand on a piece of paper. **This is how you think others perceive you.**

Now call 5 people who know you best (friends, colleagues or family) and ask them about the brand you carry.

Now compare both views- yours and theirs.

If there is a mismatch, that's your gap. Either you are over-projecting yourself to the world or you are under- projecting yourself.

In either case, people do not know you well and you need to get it right.

"Your Authenticity is your biggest competitive advantage"

– Carla Harris

How your job has worked out for the past 1, 2 or 3 decades is not how it will work out in the future. You need to be out there and stand apart from the crowd, so that your real strengths are visible in the world.

Consider your job. If your manager, their manager or the top leader knew that what you do is very good, would it not be a faster way to get the promotion or that project you want to get? Would it also not mean that you will make more money?

You **have** to work on your personal brand actively. You could be as good as you want, the best in your field, but unless the world knows about it, it does not really matter.

This is not a replacement of hard work. You still have to work hard as it creates **performance capital**. Something that represent excellence. This also means that people notice you and want to engage with you.

This Performance Capital is developed primarily by being excellent in your job. It attracts potential sponsors – who can then spend time in helping your grow.

It also means that you can get promotion, bonus, more money, etc. in the short term.

Beyond a point however, the performance capital diminishes as people expect that level of work from you all the time.

Now they expect something more. A lot of people in their early career get lost here and consider this to be the only way forward, which means constantly upgrading their technical skills and becoming better and better. But beyond a point, it becomes hard as they get to a level where other skills become more important.

Most people ignore the need to invest in **relationship capital**, which is about building connections across the organisation and across the wider industry as well.

Carla Harris, the Vice Chairperson of Morgan Stanley Bank articulates it very well. She says that all the important decisions about your career take place behind closed doors.

Unless people can vouch for you when you are not present in that room, how are you going to cut it? It is essential that you invest in genuine relationships at the right level in the organization.

Shilpa: My first promotion in a large Australian bank was literally a cakewalk. My manager told me that when my name was discussed in that room, there was no opposition and no one actually cared to see the presentation she had put together for putting my case forward.

Next one just refused to recognise me. I didn't do a good job at getting my brand out there as I was in a great project and loved keeping my head down and work. In fact, I worked longer hours than before and did a much better job than before!

I later found out that the biggest reason that it was rejected twice was because, the decision maker didn't even know who I was!

Don't make the same mistake. The only caution I will give you is, don't run after the promotion as an end objective. Run after excellence the way we talk about throughout this book. Play it full but ensure others get to know about awesome work you do.

In fact, don't rely on your organization alone. Create a vast network, where people know you for who you are and you become your own authentic brand.

How do you do that? Coming this far in the book, you already know who you are. It is a matter of letting other people know. It is not difficult to get noticed in today's world, thanks to the social media.

Leverage any tools, show yourself up authentically and consistently by putting out useful content that provides some real value and soon people will know about you.

There is only one rule. **You have to be authentic**. You fake it, it dies! You have to be completely congruent with who you are.

You may say there are constraints that do not allow you to share your brand on Linkedin or such platforms. Find out about it from your company if they have policies against you posting content that you are passionate about.

You may even worry that your passion is in some other area. Think about it, no one in the right mind will object to it, unless of course, you are badmouthing your company.

Unleash yourself because the world deserves to know your excellence and gain from it!

It is about taking your strengths, your unique capabilities, your pockets of brilliance to the world and tell them what you are bringing to the table and why should they deal with you.

Social Mastery is all about Presence, Branding, Relationships, Social Media, Networking.

Things to consider doing internally within your company:

- **No hiding** – Do not shy away from those team lunches or dinners every time, just because you have to finish up your work or because you have to leave office on time daily.

- **Use internal platforms to contribute to the environment** – You can write articles, white papers, lead initiatives which can bring value to others. Be creative.

- **Coffee Machine magic** – That coffee machine at work is there not only to make coffee but to build relationships at all levels in the organization.

Shilpa: I once got talking to a CXO level stakeholder at a coffee machine and our thought-process clicked well. Our regular interactions gave me space to learn things differently. She later went on to became my official mentor and was quite instrumental in helping me make some massive contributions that made me stand out in my portfolio.

I met another person at the coffee machine, who later became a very close friend in life. Coffee led us to become lunch time walking buddies and her hubby is my mentee today, doing an awesome job.

Things you can do that are external to your company but will give you an edge

- Find out appropriate networking events and set out a routine to attend them regularly.

- Create your own meetup group. Hosting meetups are an excellent way to let people know who you are.

- Use Social Media (Linkedin, Facebook, Instagram, Twitter, Tic Tok, etc.) to share your ideas and express yourself.

- Gone are the days when you had to wait for months to get your writeup published in newspapers or magazines. You can pull up your ideas in a jiffy and put it out there for the world to see.

- Ever thought of writing a book to establish yourself as an authority? What better way to introduce yourself than by gifting someone your book instead of your visiting card, that lands up in the bin, most of the time?

- Not a natural writer? Not a problem, make videos on topics you are passionate about and share online.

- Scared of camera? Use audios to exchange ideas. You can easily start your own podcast today. This will give you an opportunity to meet the experts in the industry and also create your own presence.

Leverage the power of Internet. It is removing all boundaries and if used wisely, can help you create absolute wonders, no matter where you are in this world.

Ensure you set adequately high standards to ensure that you play it full!

Write down 2 things that you can start doing from tomorrow. And then take MASSIVE ACTIONS.

Power of Proximity

"Surround yourself with people who challenge you, teach you, and push you to be your best self"

– Bill Gates

Another critical part of mastering your brand is the **Power of Proximity**. Being in the company of growth-oriented people will encourage you to not only exchange ideas but to push your own boundaries to achieve the desired result in life.

As per Tim Ferriss, the author of the "Tool of Titans", you become the average of 5 people you most associate with. It is absolutely essential to choose your circle wisely.

Consider this, if you are with people, who spend time mostly talking about what is wrong with the world but never actually DO something about it – would you gain in such a friend circle?

Or if the only discussion is how their jobs suck or how bad managers are or how bad companies are?

Or nothing that bad but the only purpose of their weekend is to attend parties, drink or entertainment. People who use their weekends to live their life and charge up and then slowly go through the weekdays while thinking of the weekends?

What would you become in their company?

Some would argue that this is the norm of society.

If this is the norm you are happy with, you wouldn't have reached this far in the book. The game of life, you want to play, has to be at a level, where the last few minutes of your life are filled with wonder about what you did, lives you impacted, love you showered and the contributions you made.

Steve Jobs last few words were "Wow, Wow, Wow!

It would be awesome to be able to say it and mean it!

Kapil: When I was in my weight loss journey in 2017, I got totally obsessed with (I still am, despite managing it well – I still see my weight everyday) started talking about it everywhere and found people with similar opinions and I could learn from them. My language changed, words that I used changed – I removed limiting vocabulary from my verbiage and it was just magical.

Several of my friends themselves decided their own path for healthier life style and started following through with their own weight loss. Just positive thinking wasn't the deal for any of us, we took positive actions and encouraged each other. Each of them, who felt inspired, had their own way to get there, but the end goal was the same.

Everyone I coach, starts moving forward in their health journey as well since in a very short time, they realise that their career is a part of their life and if they are not healthy, they can't possibly enjoy life.

Most of the people in their life go by the standards and rules conferred on them by their parents, grandparents and the rest of this world, handed over by generations, allowing themselves to be part of the average game.

The fact that you are reading this book shows that you belong to 5% of those individuals, who wake up one day knowing that they need not confirm to the Society's rules. They have a hidden desire to create a much better life for themselves.

How far this desire will turn into a reality, depends upon the people that you sit with. If people around you are not charged up and spend their time watching TV, Netflix, gossiping, discussing politics and news, that's what you are bound to get attracted towards.

"Stop hanging around people, who don't want to win"

– Gary Vaynerchuk

All it requires is a desire and willingness to make it work and the company of like-minded people, who are lifting each other up all the time, driving them towards their goals.

STEP 5 – TAKE FOCUSED MASSIVE ACTIONS

"Persistence overshadows even talent as the most valuable resource shaping the quality of life."

– Tony Robbins

Are you one of those people who are brimming with ideas and start new initiatives but often aren't able to see them through? Or do you know someone at work who is fantastic while working with ambiguity but falls flat in meeting simple commitments?

Shilpa: One of my mentees (let us call her Shagun – Name Changed) was going through a significantly rough patch in life as nothing in her life was working. She was unable to keep up with the demands of her work and family. She was at a severe loss to understand how to tackle it.

Her work required her to start as early as 5:30 am each day. That meant getting up at 3 AM, prepare breakfast and lunch for her husband and son, get ready, catch a train and be at office on time due to high dependency on her shift.

Because of exhaustion and sleep deprivation, Shagun couldn't perform well at work. It meant being very dissatisfied and frustrated by the time she would reach home. After picking up her child from day care, she would go home, cook, manage her child's tantrum and then sleep by 9 to get up after 6 hours! She barely had time for her husband as her husband worked long hours.

Next day, the same cycle will start. The weekends were spent in socialising and presenting this happy couple picture to the world!

End result was a very unhappy person with an unfulfilled career, an under-appreciated family life and a significant lack of self-worth.

As we started unfolding chapters of her life, Shagun realized that she had never quite understood her own role in this. The perception in her case had actually become her reality, creating the delusion that everything and everyone around her was bad. She started coaching from me and her life started moving forward bit by bit.

Week 2- She understood that she was the reason of her existence. She focused a bit more on herself and started doing meditation and yoga.

As she calmed herself mentally, she felt a lot of peace and was able to reflect back in her life and ask simple but powerful questions – that just didn't remain a side curiosity but became an honest attempt at the conversation with herself.

What was she doing? Where was she taking her life with all the problems in the world fallen squarely on her shoulders?

Week 5- With her inner peace setting in, she started getting results at home. Her picky son started responding well to the food choices as she focused on healthy food and more importantly, partnering with him to share responsibility in food decision rather than deciding for him what he wants!

She started going for a walk with her husband and started building a layer of trust and love. Her household work reduced as her husband started sharing things and also because she stopped chasing perfection!

She realized that a loving heart can do wonders rather than a bitter tongue.

Week 7- She was offered a permanent position at her work at the terms that she wanted and also got special bonus and recognition as she surpassed 160% of her target.

This was no magic. As you have seen before, how you show up in small things is how you show up in big things as well.

By the time 8 weeks were over, Shagun had a new energy level and an assurance of life that it would be as meaningful as she wanted it to be.

She learnt that life gives you what you focus on. If you notice pain, pain increases in life and if you focus on good things, life starts treating you back with more goodness.

"Focus your mind, change your reality"

– Tony Robbins

You might be dissatisfied about a lot of things in life. However, the change is possible only when you get so dissatisfied that you use that dissatisfaction to act and make a change.

All inventions in this world happened because someone was dissatisfied with the present situation and took action to start working towards correcting it.

Action is at the root of all the success in this world!

There is never any thought, any feeling EVER in the world that created a result without some productive, useful action.

One of our family friend's father was visiting Sydney a few years back. Once, during a get together at their home, some of their friends were all talking about how the situation in India is bad and something should be done by the govt.

This old gentleman is someone who has made a significant contribution to several villages in India – by writing letters to politicians and getting things done.

He couldn't take the "talk" and asked people why they shouldn't adopt their villages back in India. He excitedly told them that without spending any money, people can make a big difference just by spending time writing letters to people in charge and making them aware of the problems.

Everyone went quiet for a few seconds. But then in a short time, the conversation returned to the same topic – this time with an additional flavour of how difficult it is to really do something meaningful in India, sitting here.

This is almost like a trash talk but everyone loves it because it makes them feel strong and as if they are DOING something about it. It gives them a reason to really not do anything and feel satisfied!

Why is it that a large number of people get satisfied with this kind of an act – or lack of it?

For that, we have to understand that for every single decision or act, each of us have 3 level of mastery (this was popularised by Tony Robbins years back)

There are 3 levels at which people operate.

Level 1: Knowledge – Most people start here and then stop here. This is built on top of how our society was for hundreds of years – knowledge seekers achieved greatness in whatever villages or areas they stayed at since the world was much smaller back then. It is so ingrained in our psyche that pursuit of knowledge is still considered one of the best things to do. It is only now, it is changing!

This comes from reading books, social media, TEDX talks, podcasts and motivational videos etc.

This is Stage1.

Level 2: Connection – how do we connect with the knowledge. How does that make you feel deep down in your heart? You may know a lot of stuff, but unless you connect with it at an emotional level, most of it is just some dry fact or awareness without meaning.

For instance, you may know what it takes to build a business but you don't actually feel connected to it at deep core level. Almost all successful businesses owners feel a strong connection with what they do and the market they serve.

Level 3: Movement – This is where most people lose it. What do you DO about that knowledge and connection you have built with whatever dreams you have?

You may know that you can get promoted to that next level, and you also connect with the thought emotionally. However, it is only Actions that enable you to walk the path to that promotion.

Keep taking small steps at a time. That is the only way to crush that goal!

"Reasons are the best way to NOT do something"

– Kapil Kulshreshtha

A lot of lounge room discussions or discussions over the WhatsApp happen across level 1 and 2 but rarely at level 3!

At this stage, we would like you to pause and reflect back on your goals.

Where do you stand in terms of the above stages?

Whatever you want to achieve – how deeply are you connected with whatever your purpose or vision you have?

And last, is there that physical mastery, where you are driven to act rather than just think?

"Inaction breeds doubt and fear. Action breeds confidence and courage. If you want to conquer fear, do not sit home and think about it. Go out and get busy"

- Dale Carnegie

Tony Robbins has a process called Rapid Planning Method (or RPM in short) that talks about how you can connect **R**esults you want with the **P**urpose and fuel it with a **M**assive action plan.

The focus is on stepping through the sequence of What you want, Why you want and then create a plan to get what you want.

The below pdf covers this in details and we encourage everyone to take advantage of this free resource, this world class coach has created:

https://www.tonyrobbins.com/pdfs/Workbook-Time-of-your-Life.pdf

Imagine that you love bringing your ideas to life on a blank canvas. A new idea hits you, you walk into your art room, start to draw, progress quite well till your excitement wears off. After persisting for a while, it ends up finding its place in a closet filled with unfinished canvases.

Your sense of accomplishment will increase multi-fold if you also become a person who enjoys putting the finishing touches to your painting, and no longer stores incomplete pieces in a closet, but proudly puts them up on the wall.

Because at the end of the day, Action is where you get result from.

STEP 6 – CONVERGE AND CORRECT

"Shit changes, get used to it"

– Gary Vaynerchuk

Few years back, Malcolm Frank, Cognizant's CMO came to Australia for the first time. He gave a talk about how life in older, industrial era was more like Egg and Yolk, where the office workers were able to keep life and work separate. He added that in today's world, it is more like an omelette.

Malcolm shared this idea in 2011 – when FB was barely popular, twitter was a baby and Instagram, Pintrest, tiktok didn't even exist.

In the environment of such fast pace change, the best laid plans are not likely to succeed.

Gary Vaynerchuk, chairman of Vayner Media and world's social media guru says that he doesn't have 5-year plans for his company. In 5 years, the world would be something he cannot even imagine, he says.

Singularity University, a brain child of Peter Diamandis and Ray Kurzwell, focuses on mega industry trends across 9 areas that include, Human Lifespan, Nano-Technology, Brain, AI, 3D printing, Internet adoption in poor countries, Energy Abundance, Multi-Planetary Exploration and other associated areas. As per them in next 5 years, the technology convergence will open up doorways that currently are almost impossible to imagine except in labs around the world.

In such a scenario, what you do today and what you would end up doing in 6-12 months could be extremely different and will completely surprise you.

Unless you prepare for it today.

The entire 7 step process is built with a deep level of flexibility. The outcome is all that matters and so it does mean that you may have to go back to step 2 and adjust goals. It may even mean that you may have to develop mastery on something else by going to step 3 or take different actions to get visibility through step 4.

The change in approach, therefore is the absolutely essential to get your objective.

It is great to take actions but it is more important to be able to identify what results you are producing and if your results are not in accordance with whatever criteria of success you have put in, you would be barking up the wrong tree.

We are in for massive actions – but the actions have to converge towards a solution, intended result. That correction may even come in the form of changing the expectations or in form of doing something entirely different.

The only way to accomplish something is to Act, Measure, Get results, Correct – to ensure you are going in the right direction

Have you ever been in water splashing games in a pool or a river? Remember what we do – we keep throwing water at each other and first one to give in usually loses? Those who win are often not the smartest one but more brutal ones.

Shilpa: I always won those. But I got a lesson few years back. I was at it, and my daughter simply turned her back and kept splashing water at me – I lost.

Then I got smarter – As she turned her back – I did the same.

But she was smarter – she moved and the very next minute, came to stand in front of me! I lost again!

Don't fight the battle you can't win. Change the game.

Correction can take that kind of a form as well.

This is about re-evaluating reality as you continue on your journey, rehashing goals, making corrections, revising deadlines and make them more aligned with outcomes.

If we take the example of Shagun above, her 8 weeks journey was nothing short of spectacular

- She won her mental health,

- She felt physically much better.

- As she felt physically and mentally strong, she was able to give time to her relationships.

- As she gave time to it, her relationships flourished.

- As her relationships flourished, she found it easy to cope up with her job pressures.

- As she started finding her work easy, she flourished there and surpassed all her targets.

- As she got handle on her life, she realized that she had everything to keep her happy.

- Her happiness brought her fulfillment.

Everything in your life exists in balance with everything else. Move a chord a bit, and your life starts playing a different note.

As long as you keep correcting and adjusting the direction, you will progress.

STEP 7 – SUSTAIN THE GROWTH

"Whatever you hold in your mind on a consistent basis is exactly what you will experience in your life."

– Tony Robbins

Kapil: One of my clients in early days of coaching, a client Stan (name changed) engaged me to help him get a job. In my early days, I was still open to the short-term goals and so I helped him.

He ended up securing a great contractor role at a large company. The 7-step process was not as mature and tested back then and therefore, when he stopped the engagement, I only had an uncomfortable feeling of something missing but couldn't put my hands on what.

In about 5 months, Stan and I reengaged and this time around, there was firmness about my overall structure and method. Stan's diligence and my insights on purpose came together very well in launching his version 2.0 and has now become an unstoppable force.

He decided to start a business serving disability sector and it is incredible to see how he is now able to move the mountains. In this entire process, his challenges that he used to be concerned about have disappeared, his issues and problems he faces are now at a different level and his habits of how he prioritises has become well aligned to his purpose.

Almost everyone has the ability to start something different, pretty much the moment they become deeply aware of their beliefs and what holds them back.

Sustaining it is a different matter altogether.

Driven by your purpose, you are now in complete congruence and hopefully taking massive actions. However, if you have not developed disciplines and small habits, things may go wrong and the whole thing can get derailed.

If you have right systems, the right habits in place, so that actions become effortless. It takes literally 21 days to completely form any new habit and 66 days for it to become automatic.

If you were to do something out of the box at your workplace this week, you will have to put in a lot of thought and you may struggle even to come up with a single idea. But once you bring together your thoughts and implement one idea, you will get a taste of the feeling when you go above and beyond.

Once you get into this habit of taking a new initiative at work every month, after 2-3 months, your mind will automatically start looking for ideas to implement.

Before you know it, you will start getting more ideas than what you can practically implement and the creative juices that will flow will be very fulfilling and extremely rewarding.

In fact, this also builds abundance mindset as our mind gets focused on few things, ideas keep popping up one after the other and sharing them openly for others to build them doesn't really bother us.

"Anything that you do well is worth doing it again and again and then again."

– Kapil Kulshreshtha

The only way to continue to grow and continue to tap into your personal power that you have discovered in this book is about setting up Rituals, Habits, Actions, your circle of friendships which you can contribute to and leverage.

These are few habits that we recommend, to sustain easily and to connect everything together. Hopefully some of them you are already doing.

Dear Diary

We recommend writing a daily journal or diary. Writing down is the best way to connect and talk to yourself. In fact, in several books that refer to success habits, there is a significant mention of diary writing.

Taylor Swift, whose success is carried with a humility and contribution has several times shared images of her diaries, she has been writing as a child.

Writing your thoughts everyday creates focus and alignment in ways that cannot be easily duplicated by any other way.

However old or young you are, this can start from the day you decide to do it.

In our 30 days program that we conduct every 2 months, where attendees get 1 challenge a day, writing diary is the one of the daily tasks. Majority of the people who do the program end up making it a habit as they get significant outcomes from it.

Morning Routine:
20 min for Connecting with yourself

- Gratitude - Start your day with writing 3 things you have gratitude for. Cover different areas of the Triangle of Life, so that it doesn't become an act and you can feel it inside you.

- Write down your goals daily, with certainty and most importantly as if you are ALREADY living them – use the language "I AM". This will create deep emotional connect with them.

- Visualize your Goals – write down how it will feel when you achieve your goals. Where will you be? What will you be doing? Imagine how people will react to it? What will you be feeling? Fill in as many details into that moment as possible – all the sounds you can hear, all the emotions you can feel, everything you can see. And then, close your eyes and imagine it, live the moment, feel it, breathe it!

20 min Exercise – short simple exercises can really add up. Whatever health level you are at, start with just 10 jumping squats, 10 push-ups, 10 sit-ups and 10-star jumps. Repeat this cycle 3 times and see the magic

20 min learning – The ROI on this is incalculable. Every morning if you can immerse yourself in 20 min of audio book or podcast or a physical book reading, this will create an impetus for significant growth in your future. Y

You can use scribd or audible as platforms for books. Scribd is cheaper but doesn't have all the latest books. Audible has everything, but is comparatively expensive!

Look at your Vision Board – feel the pride of who you are and who you are committed to become.

Daylong - Anytime

- **Healthy Eating** – dieting is a sure shot way to get really bored and ultimately create a feeling of failure – instead, have everything in moderation.

- **Mindfulness** – practice to live each day as if it is your last, enjoy each moment and whatever you do – be truly present.

- **Affirmations** are a great way to tell yourself that you can do it. What you want to get, repeat it loudly 15 times at any time of the day, as if it has already happened.

Tony Robbins has a specific incantation that he repeats every day and it creates deep sense of action and purpose.

Affirmations can be very powerful, especially when you feel them while speaking. Affirmations connect you with your capability, which lead you to take actions.

Night Routine:

- Gratitude and the best thing that happened today.

We encourage you to take our 30 days challenge for doing the above every day under guided lens and if you can sustain all the above habits for a month at least, your life will transform like none before.

Things you must give up – if you want to play it big

Consistency alone won't get you – each of us is consistent in getting up in the morning, look at our whatsapp messages or facebook. A jumble of information overload, where learning is only about 1% or even less. What results it produces other than occasional connections and sharing some beautiful moments – but those are rare.

When we work with our mentees, one of the first thing they give up is the access to huge amount of useless information, that does not add any value to them. You may say that you do not engage in anything that is useless but that would be a delusion most people are in.

This delusion will disappear when you will be driven towards a purpose you set.

Conclusion: The Road Less Travelled

"If you want different results, do not do the same things"

– Albert Einstein

In your journey of life, the path you have taken is the best path you could have taken. Sure, you made some mistakes and sure, many of them didn't turn out the way you expected, but in each case, you made a choice to do something. It nudged you in a certain direction and your life was inexorably changed.

We really hope that you are happy with the decision to read this book and that you have learnt valuable lessons which you can implement by starting to walk on your own path and create your version 2.0.

Let's consider what success would look like for you with an analogy.

Consider that each of us are surrounded by dark, endless woods and the only thing you do is chop those woods to make a path for yourself.

All you have is a pair of headphones, which allow you to hear the voices of those who came before you, and of those on this journey with you.

Have you ever wondered how, in a noisy place, you can suddenly understand the person your attention is on? While listening through the headset, you focus on specific voices, specific lessons and decide what you want to do.

This is the first secret of excellence that you can achieve. Learn to focus on what matters to you: that is why you need proximity with growth-oriented people.

Based on what you hear, how you understand it and what you want, you chop your way through the woods, charting your path.

As you walk, you talk into the microphone to guide others. Those who focus on your voice then have the option to follow you in whichever way they see fit to clear their own path.

And success?

Whatever you chop at the end of your life is success.

It is the journey you go through that makes it beautiful. It is who you impact that makes it worthwhile. It is what clearings you leave for others to get inspired by that gives meaning to life.

You have come a long way. The challenges you had when you started reading this book, have been significantly altered towards exciting things rather than the dull, every day, transactional stuff that your life was surrounded by.

Let us revisit early part of the book and see what the "playing it full" will do for you. Some part of it may look like utopian but if that is not the game you want to play in life, you are missing a significant opportunity!

THE NEW WORKPLACE

You walk into the office with fire in your eyes and a dance in your steps. It is showtime! Every day, you are focused on impact and value because you are so aligned with this place. Whether it is the same office or different, you are on the go!

You can see the benefit of bringing your authenticity to work every day. And for you, this is not just a word but a way to be. The mask is gone and people see you as who you are. You also notice that this is the environment you were meant to be in, as everyone is driven by common objectives.

You are aware of your strengths as you have gone through the Gallup Strengthfinder and more importantly understood it with your coach. This has been a game changer on how you have started to leverage the best within yourself.

The politics is gone. Your busy days are replaced with highly productive days and work has become an enjoyable way you express yourself. The promotion you wanted it just around the corner but you are keenly aware of your view point that this is no longer something you are desperate for but something the organisation has to do to fuel their growth by leveraging your brilliance and allowing your growth.

You still are playing to win but with a curious difference. You are carrying everyone around you WITH you. You have been transformed into a leader – irrespective of what stage you were in your career.

You are now making more money than before simply because of your personal power. You have started putting financial plans in place for building parallel sources of income. You love your job but you want to ensure you don't depend on it entirely for your living and it has kind of taken the stress away.

The non-cooperative manager you had has now been transformed into an individual, who considers you her right-hand person and you both are deeply committed to each other's success.

You are clear about your goals in your career and have a good idea of long-term purpose you can follow.

The presentations you make are now impactful and create opportunities for your and your company's growth. You have a significant personal brand within the company and are sought after person for visible and high impact projects.

Your work environment today is collaborative, cohesive and diverse.

In such an environment, you know you are not judged for making a mistake, and collaboration is natural as you worry less about who's getting the credit and more about what you're delivering to your customers.

Your own listening for the dissenting opinion has opened pathways for others to listen to you carefully. It has allowed you to carefully weigh options before reaching a conclusion and just that act, resulted in a change in a long-held habit of jumping to defend.

THE NEW BELIEF SYSTEM

You sometimes think of how you spend a huge amount of time being limited by what you learnt from your environment in past but had never challenged. However, you don't regret any of it – you wouldn't be the person you are today without those experiences.

You discovered your story and then reached closure on it by talking to the person who you felt had wronged you. Looking back, it seems impossible to live under that weight. You are so full of joy that you don't feel limited by anything!

Your strong belief set that you created during this journey of self-discovery and growth, has been your partner throughout. You have managed to stay on course because you spend time with your coach on finding your purpose, your vision, your own personal stamp on your mission and goals. As you progressed, you were able to articulate your values and understand how you need to continue to use them as a moral compass.

All this has been possible because of the standards you have set for yourself and you constantly assess yourself against them to continue to move higher.

At the core of your heart, you feel rock solid and you know that you are slated for greatness.

YOUR FUTURE SELF

You sometimes feel surprised how you ever felt low – the feeling you have now is jubilance and freedom each day.

The brightness that you used to see around a corner earlier is now a part of your life every day. The setbacks and downtimes are there today as well but these are effervescent because you are surrounded by great people who are able to constantly challenge you to up your game and continue to be the best version of yourself.

You are unstoppable and growing each day. You can see yourself at a different level literally every month and have now a deep understanding of what it means you grow exponentially. Because you see, that is who you have become!

Just Before You Go....

TO DO LIST

"Do or Do Not. There is No Try"

- Yoda

- Join the FB page for the book "@TheBookPlayItFull".

- Share your Purpose, Vision, Mission on the @TheBookPlayItFull book fan page, let the community help you refine it and give you feedback and encouragement.

- When you discover your story – you may need help to play it back and get advice – shoot us a succinct note on FB Messenger and we can advise how to go about it.

- Share a picture of your vision board on @TheBookPlayItFull book page and inspire others.

- Expand that vision board and create a "6 months project plan" that you can stick in your house. Each month should be on a separate A4 size paper and should have the key goals you want to accomplish – financial impact and obstacles to remove. This one is a game changer for taking your execution at next level.

- Get rid of "Try" from your vocabulary. This one small change will have a very high impact.

- Get a small A5 size diary and start writing your journal.

- Refer to our personal Top 10 books

  › "You Can't Hurt Me" - by David Goggins

  › "The Code of The Extraordinary Mind" - by Vishen Lakhiani

  › "Awaken The Giant Within" - by Tony Robbins

  › "The 10X Rule" - by Grant Cardone

  › "The Grit" - by Angela Duckworth

  › "The Magic Of Thinking Big" - by David J. Schwartz

  › "F.U. Money" - by Dan Lok

  › "Own Your Day" - Aubrey Marcus

  › "Game Changer" - Dave Asprey

  › "The Power Of Broke" - Daymond John

A CHEAT SHEET TO FAIL IN THE CORPORATE WORLD

While, majority of this book deals with how to grow in your career, there are some absolute no-no when it comes to your career growth. We know that none of our readers would be in that stage where they will exhibit any of the below behaviours.

However, we decided to include this in the bonus section to help our readers understand that if they see this behaviour around them, they NEVER need to be concern about competition from such people because these people eventually lose. And when they do, they really come down crashing. The below is mentioned in a decreasing order of importance

1. **Lack of energy** – if you are not energetic, you would not make it far. All of us are passionate about things we love. Even if you do not show it, it will be seen by people.

2. **Being a taker** – you will be found out and the fall will not be pleasant. You can succeed in long term only if you are a giver who accept others to contribute to him/her as well. Do not try to "balance it" – give significantly more and when others give, take that.

3. **Lack of organisational alignment** – if you are not aligned with the organisation, you will eventually fail. People will see it through and your personal brand will get badly messed up. Similarly, talking bad about your company is never going to serve you. You need to be a problem solver and not a problem creator.

4. **Lack of client focus** – if you are not aligned with your client – it will come back to bite you very hard.

5. **Focus on money/promotion/designation alone** – a single minded focus on money will lead to comparisons with others and soon you will end up having a brand that will not be easy to shake.

6. **Focus on work in isolation without relationships** – if you are a loner, or if you just want to work in isolation – corporate environment is not for you. Companies thrive on collaboration. A loner is tolerated at best. This doesn't mean you don't have a place if you are introvert. An Introvert is not a loner. An Introvert is a massively critical part of a team.

A loner just doesn't mix with people and is a damaging element of an organisation.

Above are few behaviours to keep away from to avoid the catastrophic failure in your corporate environment. The purpose is to warn you to steer clear of these, or else the damage will negate all your hard work and impact your dreams.

PULLING IT ALL TOGETHER

"You can choose to be average. Or you can choose to be extraordinary."

- Brandon Burchard

Mike Tyson won 50 out of 58 of heavyweight title. He was the youngest of all the boxers ever to win the heavyweight championship. Despite that, at 52 now, he is recovering from a series of failures. He has finally got his life in order but in the process has hurt others a lot.

He is now a true force to reckon with because of what he is doing in promoting the sports he loved. Despite all his challenges, he has turned it around.

However, majority of us wouldn't want to follow his footsteps.

There was a greater, more sensational boxer out there, Mohammad Ali. As the greatest boxer of all the time, he was the CEO of his life!

He is the one you want to follow.

All of us are filled with wonder and awe on seeing excellence beyond norm. It is time to not sit outside the arena but to jump in. There is nothing beyond you. There is nothing "Too Big". Your focus on yourself, on your growth and on the impact you make, will open up a gateway to untold riches and wealth beyond your current imagination.

You can be extraordinary as well. All you need to do is to give yourself permission to fail - again and again and again.

With this book, our job is not done till **we ask you to commit to be the CEO of your life**.

You can do it by committing to your growth across the entire Triangle of Life and be the best version of yourself.

Own your time – own your destiny.

Be the CEO of your Life

Make a conscious choice.

Today is YOUR DAY.

Afterword

Congratulations on reading this book and taking the right steps towards playing it full in your life and your career.

We have to make a confession.

Many people would have picked up this book to get ahead in their career by following some quick strategies. Instead of that, what they got is a key message that changing their career is about changing their life.

The only sustainable change anyone can make is by making a permanent change in how they view the world and their role in it.

All the ideas in this book rotate around a central theme. Did you pick it up? Did you notice the recurring patter in every single thing we have written – for the most part?

Did you find something you were not expecting at all from a book of this nature?

If you did, we would like to hear about it at **playitfull@ scintillate.com.au**.

Furthermore, if there are any pointers that you think will help you and our other readers significantly, you can share your inputs on this mail id and we will make an effort to include this in second edition.

And if the idea is significant enough, we will even refer your name in it.

We would also love to get your review comments on the Amazon.com and the top 10 will be included in the next edition of the book.

If this book has impacted you in anyway, feel free to reach out to us on Linkedin / Facebook mentioning the word "I AM FEELING TALLER".

Remember, this is our codeword, and we would instantly feel our connection.

We look forward to hearing from you.

Acknowledgement

Being able to pour our heart & mind on this book has not been an easy journey. Like each of the great accomplishments, this one had a starting point.

It started with a simple discussion one morning in late 2018, as we both sat sipping tea in our living room, with a desire to make an impact to whoever we can reach, in every part of the world.

The biggest acknowledgement is for our beloved daughters, Sanya and Elina, who have stood strong with us as rock through the ups and downs, as we gave away a comfortable life to follow our passion and purpose.

Both of them showed insurmountable maturity at a young age of 15 and 18, as they continuously reminded us of our mission, cheering us along and with pride in their eyes.

We will never be able to thank them enough for their understanding, unwavering support, and unconditional love. In this pursuit for excellence, we became much closer together as a family, and a much stronger unit, cohesive and locked with love.

This book wouldn't have been possible without Grant Cardone's 10X Growth bootcamp in Sydney in August this year, where Grant challenged participants to stop writing their books, and finish them.

Grant became the force behind us to write this book, and as we worked relentlessly to pour our heart and soul in it, we were delighted by the most satisfying feeling of our 10X obsession, creativity, focus, action and results.

As a family of 4, the biggest influence in our life has been learning from the world's best Strategy Guru, Tony Robbins. We have adapted many of his ideas in our own philosophy of life and included them in this book for readers to consume in bite size pieces and implement.

We further acknowledge each other, our unshakeable partnership as a power couple, the insistent pursuit of our dreams and for being the biggest strength for each other.

The writing however actually started when we met Benjamin J Harvey, the Co-founder of Authentic Education, during his workshop "Difference Maker Accelerator" in Sydney. It was then, when the uniqueness of our ideas, our beliefs and the impact that we were already creating with our mentees, started to find its way in this book.

As we started the journey, constant motivation and discussions with Dev Gadhvi, India's first Passionpreneur mentor, created a momentum that we will forever be grateful for

Throughout this time period, one of the biggest supports for us came from our mentor and guide Madhusudhanan Challur, who has been a staller support through the tough times as we continued the process of building our life in this new world of prospering from our passion and purpose.

The progress continued due to constant encouragement from our close family friends, Yatin Talati, Sanjay Aggarwal and Nidhi Aggarwal and the continuous support of our siblings.

Last but not the least, the pride in the eyes of our parents and our family's openness, as we walked an unbeaten path, kept us sane and forever grateful to their belief in our dreams.

During the writing of this book, we interviewed a lot of influencers from across the globe, on our Podcast "Version 2.0 and Beyond", who added tremendous value in honing our mindset, much of it is demonstrated throughout the book as learning for readers.

These Leaders are from various walks of life and have gone above and beyond to create their version 2.0, by defying the average norm and creating their new Avatar as Influencers.

Some of these names worth mentioning are India's first blade runner and Solo Skydiver- **Major DP Singh,** Haiti based doctor, named among 12 unsung heroes by buzzfeed- **Dr Megan Coffee,** India's first Passionpreneur mentor- **Dev Gadhvi,** Melbourne based wealth strategist- **Ron Malhotra,** CEO of Alpha IT- **Bhaskar Madala,** US based financial advisor- **Michelle Machio,** Sydney based ex CIO of Newscorp and current non-executive director of Australian energy marker operator- **John Pittard,** councillor for Hills Shire Sydne- **Reena Jethi,** Melbourne based chief purpose provocateur **Mark Lebusque,** the amazing marketing guru- Edward Zia, Sunshine Coast based leader and business strategist- **Marty Vids,** the very versatile tradie chick- **Kiki Makrogianni,** US based empowerment artist and Humologist- **Rob Howze** and Brisbane based serial entrepreneur & friend **Mona Kulshrestha.**

Play It Full Program

The Play It Full Program is a 26 weeks program, where our coaches work with you on a 1-on-1 basis as your accountability partners and help you create outrageous results.

We know that something can really pump us up and then the energy just goes down. We have therefore designed this 26-week program to mindset transformation that takes our 7 step process forward and helps you create a highly contextual and personalised growth path that will change your career trajectory forever.

Reach out to us at info@scintillate.com.au for more information on how we can help you transform your life and implement the learning from this book for YOU Playing It Full...

About the Authors

S hilpa had an outstanding career in the Corporate world for 16 years with start-ups, top consultancies and financial institutions like Deloitte, Mahindra Satyam, Westpac, etc.

She was known as someone with a Midas touch and was absolutely adored by her customers, colleagues and managers, for her commitment and outstanding results.

However, life does take everyone on a roller coaster ride.

10 years down the line, the challenges of life started to show up. Kids, multi-tasking, conflicting priorities started to pull her down. As the monster of work-life balance roared loud in the corporate workplaces, gobbling up excellence for many, Shilpa found herself caught in the average game.

When she hit the lowest point in her career, Shilpa decided to pause; to reflect and evaluate where her life was going and this time, she took it as an opportunity to create a pivot in her life. This enabled her to bounce back with such intensity that she found herself at the peak- much higher than she ever was.

It was at this point that she realised that although there is a huge difference between an average, good and outstanding performer, the jump from one level to another is not difficult, if you follow a thought-through, well-structured approach and pave way to attract growth, rather than wait for it.

As a "Play it Full" coach, Shilpa emphasizes on attaining incredible results in all three aspects of a fulfilled life- Achievements, Health and Relationships.

Her mentees, who were once caught in the average game, are rocking their life today, performing at a completely different level, creating outstanding results.

Shilpa now knows the magic formula and is on a war against the average game.

This book is her effort to share this formula, this awesome sauce with the world, so that each person gets an opportunity to fly high and through a ripple effect, it creates an exceptional world.

Kapil spent 22 years in the corporate world in senior leadership positions at some of the largest organisations in the world, such as Microsoft and Cognizant.

Having worked with thousands of people and leading hundreds, Kapil has personally been responsible for the fast-paced growth of several individuals throughout his career. His passion for people's growth and insights into what it takes to grow within a complex environment came together as Scintillate, an Australian company he co-founded in 2017 along with his partner Shilpa.

Today, Kapil is on a mission to enable one million people make conscious choices to live a life of passion across all areas of their lives and discover their own version 2.0.

This current initiative of enabling people to fast track their career has transformed the lives of all of his mentees. Their continued results and growth give him deep fulfilment and fuel to continue his quest.

Kapil is known for his high energy, his genuineness and most of all for his ability to turn around any situation.